DEVOPS

*Simple and Effective Strategies
to Understand DevOps*

ETHAN THORPE

Table of Contents

iv

List of Acronyms

DevOps   Development and Operations

ENIAC   Electronic Numeric Integrator and Computer

IoT   Internet of Things

NASA   National Aeronautics and Space Administration

OS   Operating System

QA   Quality Assurance

DECUS   Digital Equipment Users' Society

XP   Extreme Programming

ITIL   Information Technology Infrastructure Library

ITSM   Information Technology Service Management

CoP   Community of Practice

CoI   Community of Interest

RCA   Root Cause Analysis

APM   Application Performance Monitoring

SLA   Service Level Agreement

IBM   International Business Machine

LAMP   Linux Apache, MySQL PHP

CLM	Collaborative Life-cycle Management
IaaS	Infrastructure as a Service
PaaS	Platform as a Service
MaaS	Management as a Service
CT	Continous Testing
CD	Continous Deployment
CI	Continous Integration
UI	User Interface
SAFe	Scaled Agile Framework
DAD	Disciplined Agile Delivery
ALM	Application Life Cycle Management.
Apps	Applications
IDE	Integrated Development Environment

Introduction

This book presents a collection of simple and effective strategies to enhance collaboration and communication among software developers and operators by using the DevOps approach. This book gives the reader the theoretical background of DevOps, DevOps principles, and practices required to successfully implement the DevOps approach and attain the desired results.

This book will appeal to people at any level of understanding of DevOps, including production managers, developers, Quality Assurance personnel, IT operations experts, information security (InfoSec) experts, as well as for customers who may need to know the processes through which their product will be designed. This book does not require the reader to have extensive knowledge of DevOps. Chapter 1 introduces the necessary terminologies and concepts needed to serve as a primer and to familiarize the reader with the terms that will be used throughout the book.

The book slowly describes the concepts of DevOps from the definition, its history to advanced tools used in the implementation of DevOps. The principles and concepts are described in a detailed and straightforward manner so that any novice can understand. At the same time, the book can be a useful reference guide for a pro-developer since it covers a wide range of simple strategies that a developer can adopt in the implementation of DevOps in the software development cycle.

DevOps methodology comprises more than just processes and tools; DevOps is a cultural movement that brings developers, IT, and organizations together to build and deploy applications in a continuous manner to deliver quality software. To implement the DevOps culture requires a change in the way the company approaches software development. It needs a culture of collaboration and continuous improvement in which all the stakeholders are involved in the development cycle.

This book will give you intricate details on how to harness and leverage DevOps culture in ways that will continue to grow and flourish with your business or organization. By understanding and executing DevOps, project teams of any magnitude can deliver quality software to their customers faster hence giving them a competitive advantage. It is exciting to see how the DevOps culture has evolved.

Let's begin the DevOps journey by first describing how this book is organized.

What is DevOps?
We introduce the fundamentals of DevOps, the definition of DevOps, and a brief history of DevOps. You will also learn how DevOps differ from outdated IT methods. You will also learn what DevOps is used for and how it can be useful to your projects. Essential concepts and terminologies used in DevOps will be defined here. You will learn what makes DevOps unique and why organizations prefer DevOps over traditional approaches. You will understand why corporates value DevOps and how the DevOps approach works. This chapter provides all the essential information

to help you understand what DevOps is and how you can apply the fundamental principles of DevOps in your daily tasks. Finally, you will be introduced to the core elements of DevOps and learn how DevOps differs from ITIL. This chapter is DevOps 101, for those who are entirely new to DevOps. Even if you know DevOps very well, we still encourage you to read this chapter as the comprehension of DevOps differs from one person to another.

Application of DevOps

We introduce the concepts of DevOps and explain what DevOps can do to increase the efficiency and speed of delivery of software. In this chapter, we will explain the lifecycle of DevOps and show you how it can be adopted for software development. Here the five stages of the DevOps cycle will be defined and discussed in detail: planning, development/testing, deployment, operation, and monitoring.

Implementing DevOps

We discuss how developers can efficiently implement DevOps software development. Additionally, you will learn how DevOps processes can be streamlined in the project life cycle and the necessary tools required for the adoption of DevOps. Steps of prediction or foreseeing challenges in software development will be discussed. The people, as a core pillar of DevOps, will be discussed and how people can work together in DevOps methodology. You will also learn the proper steps to follow to hire the right people for your organization. This chapter also introduces the appropriate feedback mechanisms for DevOps. How competition and collaboration are handled in DevOps will be emphasized in this section. By the end of this chapter, the reader will be knowledgeable about DevOps processes, DevOps implementation procedures, and its components.

This chapter introduces the reader to the tools used in DevOps, how to select the tools, communication tools in DevOps and automation tools used in DevOps. You will study the management hardware lifecycle in DevOps, artifact management, advanced DevOps tools concepts, and how to select the right tool for specific tasks.

DevOps and Cloud Computing

We explore more about how cloud computing can enhance the adoption of DevOps in various organizations. We will also delve into the deployment of full-stack and various cloud services models that can be adopted in DevOps. The reader understands how cloud services facilitate DevOps and how to handle cloud deployment. The reader will learn the right cloud model for DevOps and its various services, e.g., Infrastructure as service (IaaS) and Platform as a Service (PaaS). Finally, the reader will learn how to apply the DevOps approach to hybrid cloud services.

How DevOps Handles recent Technology Challenges

We discuss how DevOps has been able to solve recent IT challenges. For instance, how DevOps can be used in the development of mobile Apps. We will also explore the ALM processes, agile in the project cycle, how to manage multiple-tier apps. Furthermore, we will explore how DevOps can be applied to an enterprise business and supply chains. Recently, all over the world, the Internet of Things (IoT) is largely being adopted in the development of Artificially Intelligent systems. We will explore how DevOps helps developers and operators navigate the Internet of

Things (IoT). The reader will learn the role of management in DevOps implementation, the role of management in DevOps implementation, how to form DevOps teams, how to set DevOps goals. In this chapter, you will also be introduced to the lessons learned from the implementation of DevOps and how to leverage test automation in an organization. You will also learn how rapid experimentation can be incorporated in DevOps implementation, continuous improvement principles of DevOps, and lastly, we will explore DevOps results.

Nineteen Myths Surrounding DevOps

We explore the myriad misconceptions surrounding DevOps and dispels the myths that indicate that DevOps will not work in some situations. You will understand what DevOps can do and what it is not meant for.

Finally, we shares information on the future of DevOps and what readers should expect to have learned in the book.

Chapter One

What is Devops?

The acronym DevOps is a combination of two words 'Development' and 'Operations.' DevOps is simply a culture that augments communication and collaboration between software developers and operators. DevOps can be defined in many ways because it is viewed differently from a developer and operator perspective. Some may define DevOps as a software development method, while operators will look at it as tools and technologies for configuration management and continuous delivery of software development projects.

During the software development life cycle, the developer's and operators' teams' needs may differ greatly. Developers will require the features of the system to be delivered to the clients quickly while operators will insist on system stability, which involves changing the development processes more often.

Therefore, DevOps helps to reduce turnaround time for the organization to deliver projects to clients. It helps firms serve their clients better, hence increasing their overall competitive advantage. DevOps helps organizations to effectively manage the collaboration between managers and developers in the delivery of projects that can be automated or involves the repetition of particular procedures and processes. Simply put, in Information Technology (IT), DevOps acts as a seamless link between development and IT operations using efficient communication and collaboration tools.

DevOps helps to make delivery of software projects easy and seamless, using a collaborative approach between the developers and operators. To fully understand DevOps, it is important to study the history of DevOps and how it came to be.

Ideally, DevOps brings Developers and Operators together. These two people usually have different viewpoints in the project development cycle. To understand DevOps better, let's look at the varying viewpoints of the Developers vs. the Operators and how DevOps can is implemented to enhance collaboration and integration of the two.

Developer's Viewpoint

- Developers are usually supposed to work with operators to understand the nature of production systems that their application will be running on. This includes the standards of production and how the applications will perform.

- Developers should be involved in testing. Developers are required to go further and test how the code will perform in the production and ensure that the code is error-free. This means that developers should work closely with the Quality Assurance team and test the application in a production-like environment.

- Developers are required to learn how to monitor and deploy software and understand the parameters used by operators. Developers should be able to interpret processes and understand how processes interact with each other.

- Basically, developers are required to communicate and collaborate better with operators.

Operator's Viewpoint

- In the development cycle, operators should anticipate the code that is coming from the developers. This requires close collaboration with the developers right from the requirements stage of application development. This process is called Shift left, as discussed earlier on Lean methodology.

- Operators will be required to automate their systems. Automation helps the operators to achieve rapid changes with stability. Automation facilitates the handling of rapid changes and rollback in case of errors in the processes.

- Operators are required to version their systems. This is only possible if the infrastructure and the changes are captured and maintained in a version-controlled code. Hence the need for leveraging infrastructure as code.

- Operators should have monitoring systems throughout the software development cycle. Operators should be able to detect errors immediately they occur in the system.

- Operators should also communicate work closely with the developers.

This means developers and operators should strive to work together closely. The roles of each will change drastically with the adoption of DevOps. All the stakeholders involved in the software delivery lifecycle are required to communicate and collaborate better and often.

The History of DevOps

Let's delve into how DevOps came to be an inevitable component of software development. We will study the history of DevOps and how the culture has been evolving over time.

Prior to DevOps, the development and operations departments of IT worked separately. Back then, testing and deployment of systems were done in isolation, thus taking longer to deliver a project. Before DevOps, software designers used to spend a lot of time testing, deploying, and designing instead of concentrating on the actual task of building the project. This simply meant that back then, the developer was at the same time the operator.

This approach was prone to human errors since the processes were done manually. Additionally, project teams (developers and operators) had different timelines for delivery of the project; hence were unable to synchronize the project development process causing further delay in delivery of the project.

DevOps concepts date back in the '60s when the first Electronic Numeric Integrator and Computer (ENIAC) was programmed by Jean Bartik. This was followed by the adoption of a similar strategy by Margaret Hamilton of National Aeronautics and Space Administration (NASA), who was tasked to design software that would be used by the first space mission to land man on the moon. She came up with the system design approach that allowed for debugging the individual components of the system, testing the components separately before assembly, and later integrating and testing the finished system. This approach shows that the DevOps culture dates back in the '60s despite the fact that it came to take shape in the year 2009 in the first DevOps day conference.

Then came the era of the operating system, around 1979, when Usenet was started by Tom Truscott, Steve Bellovin, and Jim Ellis. The Operating system's design, concepts, and processes were held as a corporate secret back then with system administrators and engineers working as silos. There was little or no sharing of knowledge and lessons learned from problems encountered while developing the system.

As the operating systems became complex, there was a need for specialization of skills. This resulted in the formation of system administrators who specialized in managing the system and minimizing the cost implications for software. Software engineers also came up during this period to concentrate on creating new systems and features to solve new client demands. Also, Quality Analysis (QA), software security, database management, and storage became an important aspect in the design of operating systems (OS).

Then came the Internet, which made the world become one global community. Programmers and IT operators used the Internet to share ideas with each other online. User groups came up, where users of a specific technology could meet online and discuss and share notes in their respective fields. Digital Equipment Users' Society (DECUS) was one such user group that came to be in the early '60s. It was constituted by programmers who coded specifically for the DEC computers.

DECUS was made up of several chapters spanning all over the world. They held various technical conferences worldwide on software development and maintenance. In 1975, a Unix user group was formed, commonly known as USENIX that was made up of system administrators.

Even with the Internet connecting the world and allowing global sharing of knowledge, many companies were secretive about how they handle critical design processes. In order to maintain a competitive advantage, companies restricted employees from sharing information about the processes used in designing their systems.

In the year 2001, people interested in Extreme Programming (XP) were called for. A group of seventeen software engineers met in Snowbird, Utah, to XP was an Agile development designed to be responsive to the current dynamic requirements compared to previous software design methodologies that required extensive testing and pair programming. Deliberate about software development. This led to the creation of the agile movement.

Later on, in the year 2004, a man called Alistair Cockburn, who was a software developer and co-author of the Agile manifesto, came up with the three priority areas in software development, which were safety, efficiency, and habitability. The methodology was called Crystal Clear.

In 2006, Marcel Wegermann, in his attempt to bring newer and better practices to the software development field, wrote an essay that sought to apply the principles of Crystal Clear to system administration. He came up with ideas like version control for Linux operating system's /etc. directory, the pair system administration, and the operational displays. He, later on, he started the mailing list for Agile system administrators.

As the web applications became more sophisticated, more tools for sharing knowledge were invented. In the same year, 2006, Twitter became a platform of choice for system administrators, developers, and software engineers to share knowledge and processes in software development. This further reduced the gap between software developers and operators and also led to the formation of more online communities of like-minded individuals. It is within this period that Agile became the most popular methodology among the software developers.

An Agile infrastructure conference was held in 2008 by Andrew Shafer in Toronto. He was a software developer who was keen on improving the software design processes and reducing the time taken to deliver software development projects. It was during this conference that Andrew and Patrick Debois realized that there was a considerable loss of productivity when a developer switched between developmental and operational processes of system design. He would at one-time have worked with agile developers and later on switched to the operations team, thus losing lots of productive time.

A good example of DevOps at work was the migration of Flickr, a community site for photographers, from Canada to the United States. After the acquisition of Flickr by Yahoo in the year 2005. It was necessary to migrate the services and data to the US. During that time, John Allspaw was the operations manager, while Paul Hammond was in charge of the development team. It was important that the two managers work together to safely move over 3 billion photos in their server in Canada to the US. John and Paul documented all the things that they had to do together in order to achieve the migration. The collaboration and communication structures used that helped them achieve the migration was based on DevOps, a cultural change that was later replicated in many areas of software development.

In 2009, a DevOpsDay conference was held that led developers to realize the importance of DevOps and how it had been used to reduce delivery time for software projects and consequently increase efficiency in project design processes. DevOpsDay conferences were later held across the world to share the knowledge with as many developers and system administrators/ operators. Real-time communication platforms like Twitter were used to spread the message rapidly using the hashtag #devops

The rapid adoption of DevOps in large companies occurred in the year 2012 when multinationals like IBM joined the wagon with their continuous delivery system called SmartCloud Continuous Delivery. ThoughtWorks and IBM initiated knowledge sharing activities by providing consultation services to other companies intending to adopt DevOps. In April 2013, IBM acquired UrbanCode, which was a system developed using the DevOps methodology. At the same time, CA technologies also adopted DevOps in the development of Nalio.

This book will delve deeper into how DevOps has shaped the software design processes. Focusing on the processes is easier since DevOps changes how developers do things and why they do them. It is not pegged solely on the end product.

Important Concepts and Terminology in DevOps

It is important to understand the terminologies and concepts behind DevOps. Thereafter, it will be easy to introduce the techniques required to implement DevOps. In this section, we will discuss the concepts of DevOps and the ideas behind them.

Waterfall methodology – the waterfall model is a software development procedure that emphasizes on a sequential progression from one phase to the next. This model was borrowed from hardware engineering. This model is based on the fact that bugs in each phase can be addressed prior to going to the next stage. The phases were requirements specification, design, implementation, integration, testing, installation, and maintenance. The figure below is a visual representation of a waterfall model.

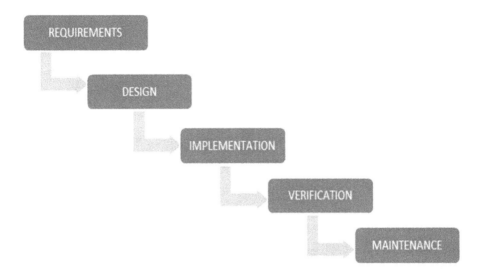

Figure 1: Representation of the waterfall model.

The waterfall model recommends a structured approach to software development. The model puts emphasis on the requirements and design stages. If the design and requirements stage is done correctly, it will considerably reduce the errors in later stages and consequently reduce the time taken in the implementation and verification stage.

This system is usually applied to software that is distributed on disks. Since once the software is sold, any fix will require selling another disk to the client. Thus, it is only prudent for the developer to get the requirement and design right in order to avoid the need for the distribution of an alternative bug fix disk.

This model is suitable for developing software whose cost of delivery is high and whose requirements are not likely to change in the near future. The waterfall model is comprised of intensive documentation, easy to understand phases, and milestones. This allows the developers to pass the project to an operator easily since the person handling the next stage can quickly go through the documentation and understand the system requirements and what to do next. Gathering the necessary information at the requirement stage can be cumbersome to a developer since the client's requirements may vary from time to time. This may cause changes in deadlines of deliverables of the requirements stage.

Extreme Programming (XP) – the extreme programming approach is typified by a five-stage sequence, namely; communication, feedback, simplicity, Courage, and respect. The model centers upon collaboration and communication between the developer and the operator.

Lean – this was borrowed from lean manufacturing. The model was meant to eliminate waste in the manufacturing process. Toyota has been known to apply this system in their production systems. The lean approach concentrates on reducing the time wasted by ensuring design consistency. The concept of Lean IT and lean software development ensures that waste brought about by unnecessary software features are eliminated. Other factors that can lead to a waste of time and resources include communication delays, slow apps response, and inefficient bureaucracy in the development process.

ITIL – Information Technology Infrastructure Library (ITIL) practices for managing Information technology services. It features processes, processes, tasks, and lists that can be applied in software development. The five core processes in ITIL include service strategy, service design, service transition, service operation, and continuous improvement of service.

Agile – initiated in the year 2001, Agile is a software design methodology that is lightweight and flexible compared to the waterfall method. Agile is a DevOps methodology that centers on individuals and interactions of the processes and tools, detailed documentation during the design cycle, client collaboration, and conforming to change while following a plan of action. Agile is a combination of various methodologies like scrum, extreme programming, and future-driven development. The methodologies emphasize collaboration and flexible designs, as stipulated in DevOps. There is a thin line between DevOps and Agile since they both focus on the people, interactions, and collaborations in software development. DevOps differ from Agile in the fact that it is a culture necessitated by historical gaps in software engineering. Also, unlike Agile, DevOps enhances collaboration and communication between developers and the Operators.

A Community of Interest (COI) – also referred to as a community of practice, are groups of developers who share a common role in an organization. The developers may have regular meetings to share notes and experiences. Each department in an organization can form a community of interest-based on the responsibilities of the department. For example, an organization can form a community of interest for the Quality Assurance department and the testing engineers, among others. A community of practice evolves as the project cycle develops. A community of practice comprises of individuals who are interested in management, governance, and communication of teams involved in the project development.

An example of a community of interest is Linux user groups. These are local groups of Linux users that meet regularly to discuss issues around Linux use, performance, database management, and propose necessary improvements and individual experiences.

Blame Culture – as the name suggests, blame culture is the tendency of blaming or punishing people when mistakes occur in the software development process. Here, the root cause is applied to establish the cause of the mistake but is blamed on one specific developer. The blame culture is common in organizations that work in silos with no transparency.

Silos – silos are used to describe people or teams that don't share knowledge with other teams or members in an organization. In a siloed working environment, people don't work toward a common goal. Project delivery in a siloed environment will be slow and prone to inconsistency and errors since the different teams use different tools and processes to achieve specific goals. The outcome from one department or team may not be a compatible input for another team since the development tools differ. Such silos prompted the creation of DevOps, which was meant to bridge the gap between developers and operators and allow them to collaborate and work together for the timely delivery of quality projects.

Root Cause Analysis (RCA) – this is a problem identification method that seeks to identify contributing factors that cause certain events and proposes relevant preventive actions to avoid recurrence. A common approach to root analysis is asking the 5-whys. This system proposes that the question of 'why?' should be asked at every stage of project development until the issue at hand is addressed or the root cause identified. The method proposes that a single root cause should be identified to aid in the project design rather than addressing symptoms of the problem.

Human Error – this is a mistake that results from a developer during the design process of the software.

Blamelessness – unlike the blame culture, blamelessness implies that a developer should derive lessons from errors instead of stopping at identifying the person to blame. Blamelessness encourages the developer to report errors and seek input from the community or managers on how to address them.

Retrospective – this is the detailed discussion of a software project which occurs after it has been accomplished. It's the stage where the developer asks themselves what went well and what aspect of the process could be improved. This can be done repeatedly during the project's life cycle.

The above terminologies and concepts defined can be put together to define further what DevOps is and how the methodologies above led to the development of DevOps.

Since we have explored the historical background of DevOps and the key terminologies and concepts used in DevOps, we will now delve deeper into understanding the applications of DevOps in software development.

What makes DevOps Unique?

Earlier in this chapter, we discussed the waterfall model of software development. We will now explore the differences between the waterfall model and DevOps and the unique features that DevOps brings.

The table below summarizes the differences between the waterfall model and DevOps:

DevOps	Waterfall Model
When a client request for software, the development, and operations teams will work together on the documentation of the new system	Upon receiving a client's order, the development team will work on testing while the operations team will work on the documentation required for the system.

Requirements and design parameters are more accurate since DevOps requires the developer to take more time to gather this information from the client.	Requirements and design parameters are skewed since the developers have little to no interaction with the client or client's specific needs.
In DevOps, the developers' team is fully aware of the progress of the operations team since they are in constant communication and work in collaboration. They will further develop a monitoring plan together using advance tools like the Application Performance Monitoring (APM) tools.	In waterfall model and other models prior to DevOps, the operations team will have no idea on the progress of the developer's team. The operations team will develop a monitoring plan that fits their deliverables, so will the operations team.
In DevOps, the application will be released in a timely manner since the developers will address any bugs during the testing stage of the project cycle and quickly fix the error.	In waterfall, if an error is made and the system fails at the testing stage, the release time will be delayed since the software has to be sent back to the relevant department for root cause analysis.

Why Organizations Prefer DevOps

You may wonder what informed the new culture of DevOps. Basically, it's evolution. From the history of DevOps and software development that we have described above, which dates back to the '60s up to the advent of the Internet in the '90s, software development can be compared to a building project that requires careful planning and activities that were planned to be executed in a sequential manner. At this point, the agile methodology came in. However, agile could not suffice the market demands. There was a need for faster delivery of quality software projects. Because of this, the agile methodology required a boost in order to deliver automated processes quickly; that is where DevOps came in to act as a launchpad for processes initially designed using Agile methodology.

DevOps was the most preferred methodology for many enterprises since it allowed Agile developers to achieve continuous integration and at the same time, allows for continuous delivery. Businesses that adopt DevOps for software development often deliver quality products in the shortest time possible, hence increasing their competitive advantage in the market.

Besides quick development, other reasons why organizations prefer using DevOps include:

- DevOps allows developers and operators to break codes into smaller chunks that can be easily managed by the teams.

- DevOps ensures companies to spend less in the software development processes hence enabling companies to compete favorably in the market.

- DevOps is based on the agile programming methodology, thus helps developers design resilient software, which is stable, highly secured, and allows for easy to track changes.

- The DevOps method reduces the risks of delivering applications that have bugs since it incorporates security checks at every stage of the software delivery lifecycle. This process helps to eliminate defects across the project life cycle.

- Since DevOps culture is based on enhanced collaboration and communication between developers and operators, the resulting products are usually of great quality compared to software designed using other methodologies.

- Mobile applications are becoming ubiquitous nowadays. DevOps allows developers to deliver projects faster, giving companies a competitive age in the highly dynamic sector of Mobile Apps. Using DevOps, enterprises reduce the turn-around time, implementation, and delivery of the project to the client.

- Products developed using DevOps are easy to maintain. Updating and troubleshooting software is easier and effortless for the end-user.

- Software designed using DevOps can be easily reproduced. It is also easy to restore software to its previous version in case of bugs affecting the updated version. The ease of use makes it a preferable approach for software development for many developers and operators alike.

- Since DevOps is based on Agile programming. Software designed using this methodology is highly predictable since it offers lower failure rates of new releases.

- DevOps approach simplifies the manual installation procedures of the organization that can be cumbersome and costly. Automation helps to improve business efficiency.

- Software developed using a DevOps approach is more resilient.

- The DevOps principles of continuous integration and continuous delivery help minimize human mistakes, reducing the time taken to implement upgrades, and facilitate productivity improvement.

In order to compete favorably in the software development market, many companies look for ways of reducing the execution gap. Adoption of the DevOps approach ensures teams are motivated since it enhances collaboration and thus saves the company from missing business opportunities.

Recently, there has been a major shift in the types of applications that companies are required to deliver; this includes:

Systems of records – earlier software applications were made of large systems that work as a system of record. This software contained large amounts of data and was stable and more reliable. Such applications do not require to be changed every time. Because of this, clients are satisfied with one or at most two releases of the software in a year.

Systems of engagement – the advent of mobile applications and the advancement in the web application have necessitated the shift from systems of records to a system of engagement that allows the client to interact with the business. But it should be noted that the system of records has not been entirely eliminated, it has only been supplemented with a system of engagement to create more robust software. Such systems are flexible and can be tweaked at any stage to address the client's changing needs and the dynamic market forces. Resultant software is usually easy to use and performs better.

Since the systems of engagement are utilized directly by the client, they require an intense focus on user experience, timely delivery, and agility. It is because of this that the DevOps approach is the most appropriate for the design and delivery of such systems.

Since systems of records and systems of engagement work hand in hand, a change in one will cause an equivalent change in the other. Such a shift is created by emerging technologies like cloud computing, Big Data, Mobile Apps, and social media, which require speedy and efficient delivery.

Understanding the Corporate Value of DevOps

The fact that DevOps uses agile and lean principles across the entire project life cycle sets it aside from other design methodologies. DevOps enables corporates to deliver projects faster by reducing the turn-around time between collecting system requirements to product release. Also, DevOps allows for the collection of customer feedback all through the product's life cycle. Feedback from the client can be used to enhance the product at every development stage.

DevOps simply improves the manner in which companies deliver value to the clients and partners hence making it an important business process in software development. DevOps offer their core values to organizations; these include:

I.   **Faster delivery** – the time value of DevOps involves developing a culture and automation that ensures fast, efficient, and reliable software delivery through the project life cycle. DevOps provides the development teams with tools for efficient planning, thus ensure projects are delivered in the shortest time possible. Different organizations will define values differently, but the adoption of DevOps ensures faster delivery of these values and a more efficient manner.

II. **Increased potential for innovation** – lean principles is applied in many organizations to encourage innovation. The primary goal of a lean approach is to minimize waste and concentrate the companies' resources on priority tasks. Lean proposes the use of the A-B test to choose the most appropriate features or capabilities that the designer should choose. Once selected, the DevOps approach is used in the design as per the selected feature.

III.   **Good customer experience** – another value of DevOps is that it's a customer-centric approach that seeks to ensure delivery of efficient systems to the customer. Once a customer is satisfied with the product, he becomes loyal to the organization and hence increased market share for the organization. DevOps approach allows developers to collect and respond to customer feedback continuously. In the current world of systems f engagement, the ability to react and respond to client's feedback with agility leads to enhanced customer experience and loyalty to the organization hence giving the company a competitive advantage.

How DevOps Approach Work

The DevOps methodology brought forth many principles that have been evolving over time. Companies apply these principles in a variety of ways that suit their business needs. In this section, we will look at how DevOps works to achieve the intended goals of collaboration between the developers and operators in software development. This is simply the application of the four principles of DevOps:

- Developing and testing against similar systems.

- Automation of repeatable processes

- Monitoring and evaluation of the operational quality

- Enhancing feedback throughout the project cycle.

1. **Developing and testing against similar systems** – this comes from a DevOps system called shift left. In this operation, the developer looks at the earlier moves in the software delivery life cycle. In this system, the quality assurance team is allowed to compare and test the current system under production with other similar systems in existence. This way, the developers can see how the application works before it is ready for implementation.

This comparison should be made very early in the project life cycle so as to allow the application to be tested in an environment that is similar to the production environment that the software will be delivered to. Also, it enables developers to test the application delivery process and validate them earlier on in the project life cycle.

This process is very useful as it enables the operators to see early in the cycle of how their destined environment would react when it handles the software application. They will, therefore, adjust the parameters accordingly to fit the intended environment.

2. **Automation of repeatable processes -** this principle of DevOps allows the developers and operators to implement

an agile process through the development cycle. The principle proposes automation to handle processes that are highly repeatable and frequent so that the organization can develop a model that allows for continuous automated deployment and testing. Automation allows the developers to test the deployment processes at all stages hence reducing the risk of errors at the final deployment stage.

3. **Monitoring and evaluation of operational quality** – businesses have tools that capture system metrics as they happen. This is an efficient monitoring tool that can assist developers in tracking changes in resultant systems. Unfortunately, this is sometimes done in the siloed working environment hence reducing the efficiency of project delivery. This principle of DevOps moves monitoring activities to the early stages of the project life cycle by recommending that automated testing to be carried out early in the life cycle to monitor functional and non-functional features of the system. Every time the system is tested, quality parameters should be recorded and analyzed thoroughly. Constant monitoring ensures that operational issues are captured and dealt with early in the project life cycle. The data collected for monitoring should be captured in a manner that all the stakeholders in the project can understand and utilize.

4. **Enhancing feedback throughout the project life cycle** – one of the key advantages of DevOps is that it allows developers to react and make relevant changes in systems

quickly. It is important for the developer to get quick feedback and derive lessons quick from every action taken. To achieve this, the developer's team is required to establish communication channels that will allow all the stakeholders involved in the project to get and act on the feedback collected. Developers will act by altering project plans or project priorities while the production team will act by adjusting the production environment to fit the project development. The organization will act on feedback by adjusting the project release plans.

Core Elements of DevOps

DevOps should not be seen as a framework; it is basically a combination of good practices. DevOps brings several good practices together to create a cultural movement. DevOps can be applied at any stage of software development today.

Common elements that enable the implementation of DevOps culture are:

- People

- Process and

- Technology

These three elements are the enablers in DevOps culture. When the three elements come together in synergy, an organization will be able to realize the benefits of implementing DevOps. To change the culture of an organization, you will need people, and these people cannot operate without set processes. When we have people and processes working together, we will have achieved the functional design to implement DevOps. Now the next question is how to increase efficiency. Human beings are prone to mistakes in handling basic processes. In order to have the processes running faster, smoothly, and efficiently we need technology to help people achieve the objectives of the processes.

It is important to note that all the three elements of people, process and technology are vital to build the DevOps methodology and achieve the project objectives.

How does DevOps differ from ITIL

Information Technology Infrastructure Library (ITIL) is a popular framework for delivering IT services. It dates back before DevOps. It was the framework of choice for service-based organizations. ITIL provided guidance on how services can be defined, developed, operated, and built. ITIL framework is made up of a detailed lifecycle of phases from inception to operation in a sequential manner.

ITIL is considered as a heavy or lengthy approach for software development. ITIL framework takes long to set up. It can take an organization over one year to set up, depending on the volume and complexity of the project.

Traditionally, software development was handled by the Software Delivery lifecycle (SDLC) approach and managed using the waterfall approach of project management. Operationally, ITIL took over. Using DevOps, development, and operations were brought together to form a union. In this union, the waterfall approach gave way to Agile methodologies, and still, developers who used DevOps processes did not have a good grasp of the ITIL concepts. This section explores the symbiotic relationship between DevOps and ITIL and why DevOps cannot exist in its entirety without borrowing from the ITIL framework.

Nowadays, ITIL and DevOps are used in synergy to develop quality software quickly. The IT industry is at any time working on the provision of either services or products. Products are the physical deliverables of IT, whereas services are intangible commodities offered by IT.

Chapter Two

Application of DevOps

In this chapter, we will introduce the concepts of DevOps and what DevOps can actually do. In this chapter, we will understand the architecture of DevOps and how it can be adopted for software development.

DevOps has broad applications that cut across the entire project delivery life cycle. Companies choose a specific methodology based on their specific objectives, goals, the issue being addressed, and the necessary gaps that require to be filled in the software delivery. Therefore, this chapter details various ways that businesses can adopt DevOps and also explains the stages of DevOps.

The Life Cycle of DevOps

DevOps represent an enhanced collaboration between the developers and the operation's team in project delivery. To better understand DevOps, one must know the stages/life cycle of DevOps. The stages in the life cycle represent the core capabilities that DevOps is supposed to provide.

The Stages in DevOps include:

- Planning

- Development or Testing

- Deployment

- Operation

- Monitoring

The above stages are the reference model or template for the implementation of the DevOps culture in an organization. It is a simple reference guide for developers, operators, executives, and other stakeholders in the project to understand the processes and technologies employed in the software development cycle.

Below is the detailed explanation of each of the stages in the DevOps life cycle:

1. **Planning** – this stage focuses on setting objectives and adjusting them based on the inputs from the customer. Also referred to as a continuous business planning stage. It is important for organizations to respond quickly to customer's feedback in order to gain a competitive advantage in the market. In order to achieve this, an organization has to do thorough planning before the execution of projects.

   Outdated approaches to software development cannot achieve this since they were based on teams working in silos. The speed of doing business today requires that teams work in collaboration with each other to quickly deliver projects. In the past, the information required to plan was inconsistent. The feedback was not received in time for the developers to achieve the right quality of software. Whereas in some old models, planning was seen to slow down the software development process.

In order to deliver projects quickly, thorough planning and agility are necessary at this stage. This is where DevOps methodology comes in to bring the developers and operator's team together to work collaboratively to set project objectives. Even at the planning stage, developers should continuously collect feedback from the customer in order to improve agility and project outcomes in a cost-efficient manner. DevOps allows the teams to minimize wastes in the planning process.

2. **Development / Testing** – at this stage, the development of the system is done continuously. At this stage, the development process is divided into smaller chunks for speedy development and delivery. At the same stage, the Quality Assurance (QA) team will apply appropriate tools to identify and fix errors or bugs in the code. This stage brings together the teams to collaboratively develop the codes while continuously testing for code integrity and quality.

At this stage, all the stakeholders are brought on board, i.e., customers, managers, analysts, software engineers, developers, QA team, operation team, security personnel, suppliers, and other partners interested in the project. A common platform is created that brings together all the stakeholders to work on the project. At this stage, continuous integration is applied whereby developers will continuously integrate their work and those of their colleagues or team members.

Continuous integration was popularized by the Agile movement. Continuous integration advocates for developers and operators to continuously integrate their work and test at each and every stage. Continuous integration and testing allow the developers to capture design issues early in development and address them timely.

Testing the codes on the go have several objectives; for example, it enables continuous verification of codes, it helps to validate the codes generated by different teams to ensure code integrity. Codes should be tested throughout the project life cycle to ensure bugs are timely addressed before passing the project to the next development stage. To make this process faster, the process is often automated to handle repetitive tasks.

3. **Deployment** – at this stage, the developers will continuously deploy the codes created. Deployment is usually done carefully in order to avoid compromising the functionality of the primary system. Deployment is a very important stage in DevOps since it further enhances continuous integration. Continuous deployment ensures that the customer gets the latest features continuously through the project life cycle.

    DevOps approach is centered on continuous integration, continuous-release, and continuous deployment.

4. **Operation** – this stage comprises continuous monitoring of the codes designed and continuous collection of feedback from the customer to assist in the optimization of the system to conform

to customer requirements. At the operations stage, customer's feedback is very important in system optimization. Feedback tools will be used to capture customer feedback and allow the responsible teams to take action to improve the system. DevOps allows for this continuous feedback loop that ensures agility in running the business and that it efficiently addresses the customer's needs.

5. **Monitoring** – at this stage, the operations team will analyze the behavior of the new codes while at the same time handle errors or bugs that may occur in the code. Monitoring is an important component of DevOps since it allows developers to deliver stable systems. The continuous monitoring approach provides parameters to the operations and QA teams and other stakeholders in the project delivery cycle.

Chapter Three

Implementing DevOps

In this chapter, we explore how developers can efficiently implement DevOps in software development. Additionally, we will learn how DevOps processes can be streamlined in the project life cycle and the necessary tools required for the adoption of the DevOps methodology.

Implementing DevOps requires one to bring together all the stakeholders. DevOps enhances collaboration, and therefore, to implement it, one will require a plan that will bring together teams, processes, and the technology to be used. In this chapter, we will discuss more on how to work with the three collaboratively to achieve project objectives. A complete implementation of DevOps means all the stakeholders, both internal and external, to the project have been brought onboard and a common communication and integration platform used to ensure everyone is updated on the progress of other team members.

Implementation of DevOps means creating the appropriate culture, identifying the organization's needs, and continuously solving errors that may occur during the implementation cycle.

Implementing a good DevOps strategy, an organization will offer many benefits like helping the organization to channel its energy and resources to high impact issues, identify opportunities for growth, and facilitate good business outputs.

An organization will implement DevOps to address specific issues like;

- Handling machine learning projects.

- Handle big data and social media projects

- For virtualization, load balancing, and containerization.

- For continuous integration and deployment

- For automating code repositories, testing, workflows, and testing.

- To perform automation of infrastructure and workflow configuration management.

There are several open-source tools that can be used in the implementation of DevOps. Some of the tools include:

- Github – is an open-source version control system. Github is web-based and hosted for GIT repositories. It allows developers to host remote Git repositories and has community-based services for the design of open-source projects.

- Puppet and Chef – these are agent-based pull systems for handling deployment automation tasks.

- Ansible – is used for automation of the software provision processes, application deployment, and configuration management, secured shell (SSH) model, playbook, and Yum scripts are the mechanisms used.

- Jenkins – this is a web-based tool used via application or webservers like Tomcat to facilitate continuous build, testing, and deployment. Jenkins is integrated with tools for building like Ant/Maven and the source code repository Git. It's comprised of master and dump slaves.

- Kubernetes – is an open-source instrumentation system for Docker containers. It categorizes containers into logical to enable easy management and discovery. It handles scheduling on nodes.

- Dockers – is made up of packaging and application and its dependencies in one pack. It handles an isolated process on the host OS and shares the kernel with another container. Docker benefits from resource isolation and allocation benefits such as VMs while, at the same time, it's portable and efficient.

Listing Organization's Objectives

Before implementing DevOps, it is important for the organization to ensure everyone understands the project requirements and expectations. The managers should ensure that the project team members have a common understanding of the timelines, reporting lines, tools, and the processes necessary for the delivery of the software.

When the team members are aware of what is expected of them and how their progress will be measured, fewer or no conflicts will arise during the actual design of the software.

Once these organizational objectives have been set, the DevOps approach will help the team members to achieve the objectives.

Foreseeing Challenges in the Software Development Cycle

Developers can meet different challenges during the project design cycle. These challenges can be categorized as:

- Communication breakdown – these occur when the developers have to convey the same information to the teams repeatedly.

- Back and forth relay of information on bugs that occur at the testing stage. This forces the team to send the codes back to the development to be reworked.

- Over design – sometimes, the developers may add unnecessary functions to the software.

- Development tools – DevOps approach is the most preferred methodology since it ensures the project is delivered faster. But since the delivery relies on tools and infrastructures that may pose challenges during implementation.

In order to avoid backlogs in the software development cycle, developers should ensure the throughput of each process is equal. In order to achieve this, the developer must routinely evaluate the processes at each stage of the cycle, optimize the pending tasks, and adjust accordingly to ensure the project meets the set objectives.

As mentioned earlier in this section, implementing DevOps requires bringing together the three main components, namely:

- The teams or people who implement DevOps.

- The Process to be followed in DevOps.

- The tools or technologies required to implement DevOps.

In this section of the book, we will discuss each of the above components in detail and how they can be put together in the implementation of the DevOps culture. We will start with the key driver of DevOps culture, and that is the 'People working in DevOps.'

People Implementing DevOps

In this section, we will be able to appreciate the people aspect of implementing DevOps and establishing the DevOps culture.

In chapter 1, we defined DevOps as a cultural movement; that means it is centered upon people. An organization may have the best tools necessary for executing a task, but if they don't have the right people to execute, they may not achieve the project objectives.

Therefore, for DevOps to work for you, you must build the DevOps culture in the people working in the organization.

The DevOps culture advocates intensive collaboration between the business rather than a specific department/silo within the organization. Implementing DevOps means continuous learning for the Developer's team and operations teams alike.

Building a culture is not an easy task since it requires social engineering of the people working on the project. Generally, people have varying levels of experience and view of things. In order to make all of them think in the same direction for a common goal, you will require to work hard on building the culture. This may pose challenges in the process since it is easier said than done.

As discussed earlier, under the concepts of DevOps, a lean and agile approach can be incorporated in the implementation of DevOps. If the business has already implemented tools like Discipline Agile Delivery (DAD) or Scaled Agile Framework (SAFe), it will be easy for such an organization to implement DevOps culture.

Implementing DevOps requires the management of the organization to work in close collaboration with the teams and stakeholders in close communication to create the DevOps culture. The teams should be sharing information and progress updates constantly in order to achieve the tenets of DevOps.

It is important to change the attitude of the people in order to achieve a DevOps culture. Attitude change may be hard to achieve in the entire team. Thus, the managers should only work with those developers and operators who conform to the tenets of DevOps culture.

Teamwork is an important enabler for DevOps to thrive in an organization. Complex projects may require several teams working together in collaboration to achieve specific objectives of the project. Teams may work separately but with continuous integration, feedback, and sharing information amongst each other. Once a team is formed and the DevOps culture instilled in them, it is important to allow the team to work on the task solely without adding other levels of bureaucracy or complicated reporting lines since that may kill the DevOps culture. No team or group of members should be seen to be superior to others during the software development cycle.

People Working Together

DevOps encourages collaboration, where people work together. But what makes people work together? This section will explore the factors that can enhance collaboration when implementing the DevOps methodology.

DevOps teams are constituted by individuals working together for a common goal. In this section, we will also study the human factors that enhance or inhibits collaboration. We will look at the strategies for achieving effective communication and collaborative work in the DevOps approach.

People are the most important component of DevOps; you will be able to understand the factors that motivate people and how people work in order to achieve DevOps set objectives.

When people work together as a team, they must have shared goals. A project cycle will be affected negatively if the team members are not working towards a common goal. The goal is usually set by the team managers who may have different individual goals compared to the teams.

Some individuals consider their current position very important in their career progression, while others look at it just as a job to support their families. The former will put more serious work on the task at hand.

People would wish to learn and grow their skills, but this greatly varies from one person to another. Junior workers would love to get as much experience and learning as they possibly can, whereas the senior employees would take leadership roles. Some people concentrate on working on specific tasks, while some prefer working on a wide variety of assignments to grow their network. DevOps approach requires that a team should have a diversity of people with varying levels of creativity, problem-solving abilities, and productivity. Although such differences often lead to inter-personal differences amongst people of different backgrounds, either personally or professionally.

When a person moves from one company of smaller size to a larger company, there is bound to be cultural differences and expectations to overcome. Ideally, people working in teams should be able to learn from each other and reduce the cultural differences that may occur. In a collaborative approach, as proposed by DevOps, the contributions and ideas from a person with more experience in software development would be considered for how easily they can be applied to benefit the entire team working on a project.

How technical an individual is or not techy can create differences amongst teams. In a company context, engineers are seen as being more important to the company and teams like support, marketing, and sales considered second in command. When such a view is mirrored by the management, the non-technical team may lose morale because they will feel their contribution to the company is not appreciated. People should be made to feel that their job is appreciated. When designing complex systems using the DevOps approach, several teams may be working on specific components of the software. The teams are comprised of people of varying professions and capabilities. Each stage of the design process utilizes the different skills of the people.

In software development processes, IT roles, for example, network admins, operations engineers, and database admins, are usually treated as being on the same level. The Operations teams are usually considered a second priority or often noticed when there had been a system break down. The DevOps culture was established because of these differences. It was meant to enhance collaboration between these teams and encourage effective communication to eliminate such differences.

Even among the technical teams, there may exist differences in individuals' backgrounds. To diversify an engineering or technical staff working on a project or a company, continuous training should be encouraged for the staff.

Another important aspect of the people that should be considered when implementing DevOps is the working style of the developers and operators working on the project. The personal and professional background may affect how individuals collaborated in DevOps projects. The different working styles include introverts, extroverts, asker, guessers, starter, finisher, analytic thinker, Lateral Thinkers, purist and pragmatists, night owls, and early birds.

These working styles may differ in many ways, with people falling anywhere along the scale. Below is a detailed discussion that compares the different working styles:

Early Bird versus Night Bird – people working on DevOps project may differ in their working habits based on when they feel more productive. The early birds will prefer to come to the office early in the morning before others come and do productive work. While the night bird prefers working late in the evening. When implementing DevOps, it is important to allow the developers and operators to work during hours that they consider optimum for them.

Pragmatist versus Purist – when considering engineering challenges, a purist would wish to use the best technology to address a challenge. If such technology doesn't exist, they will create one. Purists will not work with technologies that need workarounds and that they feel may compromise some engineering principles of the system. On the other hand, pragmatists are keen on the practicality of the technology and the cost benefits for creating an ideal solution versus working with existing technology and its constraints. Pragmatists will concentrate on delivering the project in its existing environment instead of creating unique technology to achieve the same.

Lateral thinker versus Analytic Thinker – A lateral thinker will seek info indirectly in order to find the missing pieces; he will examine the challenges from many perspectives and eliminate stereotypical ways of thinking, whereas an analytical thinker will focus on facts that have evidence. An analytical thinker will try to split complex things into smaller chunks and eliminate unnecessary information or worthless alternatives.

Finisher versus Starter – Finishers are people who like dealing with loose ends in projects by fixing pending issues in projects. Finishers don't like leaving things hanging or with fringes that can be repaired or completely eliminated. In DevOps, finishers are mostly found in the operations team, where they handle the final touches for an operationally sound system.

On the other hand, a starter is a person who appreciates creating new ideas, and getting them started from scratch. They are motivated by the fact that they are required to start a process from the start. Starters like testing new technologies, tweaking existing codes in many ways, and seeking new challenges to handle. But once the project is underway, they become bored, leaving the remaining tasks to be handled by the finishers.

Guesser versus Asker – a guesser, is a person who will analyze a situation deeper and will not ask questions unless they are sure of a 'yes' answer. Whereas an asker is a person, who thinks that it is ok to ask for everything since they know there can be a 'no' answer. Guessers are passive people and often indirect, whereas askers are more presumptuous. In order to efficiently implement DevOps, the managers must be well aware of these differences in personality while designing the communication plan for the project.

Extrovert versus Introvert – these are personalities that are based on peoples' energy reserves and how they dispense them. An extrovert derives energy by being around and interacting with others while introvert derives energy by being alone or in smaller and closed groups of people. In DevOps, extroverts will prefer working on group projects while introverts will prefer working in closed offices with little or no interaction with other people.

While implementing DevOps, it is important to have a mixture of these personalities. A team that is made up of a mixture of starters will be good at inventing new products and designing them from scratch. A team made up of purist only will not achieve much since they will always feel that it doesn't meet their set standards. This is where pragmatists come in to ensure they have achieved something by the next deadline.

An important step to enhance collaboration in DevOps is to allow the people working on the project to self-assess their personalities to know their personalities. The manager will then find changes that they will need to make in terms of assigning people tasks.

Working with different personalities in a project is bound to conflicts. For example, purists and pragmatists will differ in the amounts of details in project planning meetings. It is important for DevOps managers to create and maintain an environment that can support people of different personalities.

DevOps culture encourages individual growth by creating a work environment that encourages people to grow. Individual growth is very important for efficient collaboration in the workplace. It is important that workers are encouraged to have the right mindset that will enable them to grow in their respective areas of work.

People with a fixed mindset believe in the innate nature of their talents, whereas individuals with a growth mindset see talents and abilities as things that they can learn and perfect with practice. A proper mindset can have a positive impact on the project at hand since it affects how they approach challenges and how they deal with challenges and faults that may occur during the software development cycle.

A fixed mindset is detrimental to the project since it makes people think that they are supposed to prove themselves to other team members. This may lead to miscommunication and a lack of collaboration in the implementation of the DevOps approach. People with a fixed mindset are often negative. They will think they are not smart enough or talented to handle a specific task. At this stage, it is hard for a fixed mindset individual to pick new skills on the project, which reduces their likelihood of being hired.

Having a growth mindset is beneficial to the project since people with a growth mindset gladly offer themselves to learning opportunities. An individual with a growth mindset believes that his skills and knowledge of the process will grow over time. For them, challenges are viewed as learning opportunities for new skills and knowledge. They consider failure as a learning process and endeavor to derive lessons from any failures.

Hiring the Right DevOps Staff

In the previous section was centered on understanding the different personalities of people implementing DevOps. In this section, we will explore an important step in the implementation of DevOps, which is actually hiring these people.

The management should be able to hire the right people to implement DevOps. We will examine the hiring practices and how to optimize the hiring and interview processes and study ways of improving the hiring processes for DevOps staff. In this section, we will cover the hiring goals, interviewing techniques unique to DevOps personnel, and retention of developers and operators in an organization.

Identifying Hiring Needs

The first step of hiring is to determine the minimum requirements for the candidates to perform a specific task or set of tasks. There are several factors that you will consider here. With short timelines to search for talent or a small window for open job requisitions and a constrained budget, it will be tempting to spend less time on scrutinizing needs and move on hurriedly to interview candidates. It is advisable to spend some more time to find out what exactly you need to complement your existing team.

Position and skills – some skillsets are well defined. For instance, if you are using python programming language, it will be obvious that you will need to hire experienced Python programmers. It is important also to consider the technologies that a candidate is conversant with or has used prior. The position to be filled and the reasons why it should be filled will influence the kind of skills that will fit the job. If you need someone to fill a role for a specific project, it will make sense to find someone who has experience and a specific skill set for the project. This will minimize the costs incurred to train someone who has no specific experience in that field.

If you have no constraints, you can broadly search for a candidate who will fit your team perfectly. Even on cases where you need a specific skill set, like an operator who vast experience of cloud-based architectures and you are required to start hiring data center experts and network specialists, with a practical amount of time, you can be flexible as to how you source for those skillsets.

You should first check your current team for an individual interested in the position, consider whether they can fill the position if trained. Alternatively, you should also consider an employee on a lower rank that would wish to grow his skills and position to take up the job.

Considering our python example, if you hire someone who worked with python program before, but he/she has a bad culture fit or lacks some critical thinking skills, they will not fit in the DevOps methodology hence forcing you to switch approaches in future. On the other hand, if you get a good python programmer with great people and learning skills, his or her ability to learn new technologies will be high, thus a better fit for the DevOps approach.

Timeline – most organizations will not have the luxury of time for hiring new staff. The hiring because of competing tasks, the hiring process usually have specific timeframes and deadlines that should be strictly adhered to. Often times, organizations will not employ young people so as to avoid training them on specific skills. Time consideration covers situations where a candidate indicates that he prefers working with startups. Thus, if your organization grows, you will be required to replace the employee and find one that fits the current needs of the organization. This kind of turnover is time-consuming and costly. And if it can be avoided earlier in the hiring process, the better.

Budget and resources – budget constraints dictate the number of employees you will hire and the level of skills you can afford. You should be able to match the competitive market rate of the job in your area. In cases where you cannot match salaries offered by bigger companies, the startup will consider offering flexible working hours, opportunities to work remotely, among other benefits.

Sourcing for Suitable Candidates

Once you have laid down the requirements you want in a candidate. The next step is where to get a suitable candidate. Nowadays, job boards are the most suitable sourcing avenue for potential candidates. For example, monster and Overflow careers are an example of highly sort after job boards with active candidates seeking jobs.

The job seeker and the employee will create a profile on the website. The websites usually have some questions that will help in eliminating candidates, depending on how they answer the questions.

Employee Diversity

Organizations nowadays seek to employ a diverse team in the software development field. Diversity is critical for team performance, with varying ideas, perspectives, and viewpoints coming from people with different backgrounds. This is a recipe for coming up with new ideas. A diverse team will deliver products that will cater to a wide range of clients. The more diverse a team is, the more creative they will become since they will share a bunch of new ideas based on their different backgrounds.

People and Feedback Mechanisms

The quality of feedback given to individuals working on a project is a key factor in the kind of mindset that the individuals will adopt. If someone is complimented for doing something good, it makes them have a fixed mindset, thus barring them from taking up challenging tasks. Success in a project should be tied on efforts so that the person can realize that it's as a result of his or her efforts and not innate personal quality. This will encourage them to take up new challenges in future projects.

While reviewing the performance of people working on DevOps projects, it is important to keep this in mind. A feedback mechanism should be structured in a manner that allows people to have a growth mindset.

How frequent and formal feedback is, plays a huge role in creating an environment that encourages collaboration. Coupled with continuous reviews, the feedback mechanism should be designed to be regular.

Competition vs. Collaboration in DevOps

To achieve the full value of DevOps, the managers should create a work environment that encourages collaboration instead of competition. It is important to note that competition occurs when project resources that multiple team members need are scarce. The managers should encourage collaboration by efficiently facilitating the team members to share the available resources and strengthen the communication lines between them.

Communication as an Enabler for Collaboration

In order to enhance collaboration in a project or workplace, it is important to have an efficient communication plan in place. Communication is meant to create a common understanding of what someone or a team expects. Communication enables developers and operators to have a clear understanding of the technical aspects and expectations of a process. It is important to instill a culture that encourages constant communication amongst project members and teams alike.

When a developer understands a particular process very well, it is important that they disseminate the knowledge to all project members and encourage learning. Without proper dissemination, there is a risk of creating knowledge islands that can be detrimental to the timely delivery of projects. Communication is a good way to grow people's skills in an organization and encourage learning at all stages of project development.

Communication can influence people by getting them to understand your point of view on a specific design aspect of the project, thus reducing cases of disagreement or conflicting viewpoints.

Effective communication can build communities. It helps build strong teams with great empathy, creative, and very productive. Teams that communicate freely tend to work together more efficiently and can handle complicated tasks together, thus achieving excellent results. Team members should be able to communicate face to face rather than using emails. Therefore, a communication plan should be designed that allows members to have sitting meetings and encourage regular interaction amongst the project members.

Having a communication plan that caters for all project members is a key element of DevOps. Effective communication ensures that the developers, operators, and QA team are working towards the same goal and that their action is well aligned to the project requirements defined earlier in the project design stage.

DevOps Processes

Now that we have discussed the important role that people play in the implementation of DevOps, we will next discuss the processes involve in DevOps. Processes are basically what he people to achieve the project objectives or deliverables.

It is possible to instill the DevOps culture into the people, but at the same time, care must be taken to ensure the people are using the right tools and following the right processes in the implementation of DevOps. Failure to do so will lead to inefficiency in the project cycle.

DevOps is constituted of many processes; in this section, we will discuss some of the main processes in the implementation of DevOps in any business enterprise.

Business processes – DevOps approach will impact the entire business in one way or the other. Business processes define the agility of an organization and improve service delivery to clients. All business processes are usually geared towards customer satisfaction. DevOps can be considered as a business process or task implemented in order to produce a service or a product for the end-user or customer.

In chapter 2, we looked at the DevOps life cycle, which is a reference manual for developers when implementing DevOps. From the cycle, we can establish that DevOps business prosses involves handling concepts from ideation stage as stipulated by the organization through to the development and testing and later to the production and deployment stage.

Change management process – this can be defined as a group of activities designed to regulate, accomplish, and track change by recognizing the job products that may change and the necessary processes used to achieve the change. Change management is an important component of DevOps. Change management dictates how DevOps method can be applied to handle change requests and customer's feedback.

Business enterprises that have implemented the Application Life Cycle Management (ALM) have an automated process for responding to change requests.

Change management is made up of processes that enable the organization to achieve the following:

- Role-based access control.

- Planning

- Configuration management

- Dynamic workflows

- Project tasks management

Old methods of change management focused on change requests or management of defects with less focus on tracing the activities between the change requests and the requirements of the new code.

This approach doesn't utilize an integrated work-item / project task management in the project life cycle. DevOps, on the other hand, requires that the stakeholders are able to read and join forces in achieving all changes across the software development cycle.

DevOps usually include processes that enable the organization to easily link project tasks (work items) to project assets and other resultant work items. These processes allow for agile project development and give project members and stakeholders access based on their specific roles.

DevOps Implementation Procedures

To implement DevOps, the developer or operator must consider the following six techniques or procedures.

I.   Continuous improvement – as instigated by the lean-approach.

II.   Release planning

III. Continuous integration (CI).

IV.   Continuous Delivery (CD).

V.   Continuous Testing (CT)

VI.   Continuous feedback and monitoring mechanism.

Continuous improvement – the lean approach states that implementing a model or process is not an event that is done on-time, rather it should be an on-going or continuous process.

Organizations should be able to learn from the processes it has implemented continuously. A process improvement team should be put in place to derive lessons by analyzing the ongoing and previous processes.

Implementing DevOps in itself is not a one-time event; it's a continuous undertaking. DevOps proposes three important sectors for improvement, namely;

The software – these are the application changes that you have just delivered. You should be able to establish whether they are functioning properly as envisaged in the design. An organization should learn from feedback so as to improve the next cycle of development.

Development environment – the organization should learn from the environments in which the application is running on by establishing whether the environment is functioning as desired.

Development processes – the organization should be able to derive lessons learned from the entire project delivery process. Lessons learned will be used to improve the delivery of future projects.

Release Planning – this is an important component of DevOps that allows the organization to give specific timelines to customers based on business needs. It is important for organizations to have clear roadmaps in project implementation in order to better manage the development processes. Many organizations achieve this by holding routine meetings for updating the customers and other stakeholders on the progress and specific timelines of the project's processes.

Continuous integration (CI) – constant integration of processes in software development allows the developers to deliver the project in an agile manner. Delivery of a project nowadays requires many teams of developers and operators working on different components of the software. At the same time, once the application is delivered, it needs to work well with other applications and services

Continuous Integration allows teams working on a different process to collaborate and share progress routinely in order to achieve a common goal and have a common understanding of the project's objectives at each stage of implementation.

This is the process of integrating the new code that has been written by the developer with the existing or master code repeatedly through the project cycle. DevOps encourages the development team to constantly integrate the code during development as opposed to doing it when the coding has been finished. Delaying the integration to the end is prone to errors and faults that will cost the team a lot of time to address and compromise on code and software quality. In complex projects, it is difficult to separate and identify the sources of the error. With smaller chunks of codes, it is easier to find and resolve errors that may occur.

CI systems will frequently run tests automatically to confirm code integrity upon merging new codes with the master codes. Once the merging is completed, the code will run in the background to reduce the chances of the developer forgetting to initiate the process upon merging a new set of codes. The system will show a green light to indicated successful integration and red light if an error occurs during integration. Such a workflow ensures that the system problem is identified early and fixed faster.

Continuous Integration also ensures that the work of the developer's team is constantly integrated with that of the operation's team. Once integrated, the processes are validated by the Quality Assurance team for compliance to the set business objectives. Constant integration and integrity checks ensure that the process is fault-free since the developers are able to identify problems earlier in the development cycle before they affect the project's delivery timelines.

Integration is a complex and important task in the software development cycle and is a key principle from both Agile and DevOps. In the past, integration was considered after the application has been completely developed. This meant defects would be discovered late.

Components of Continuous Integration

- **Maintaining a single-source repository** – it is important to use version management tools to manage the source base that allows multi-user access, merging, and streaming that allows several developers in a remote location to work on the files. Thus, using a common platform is important.

- **Automation of build** – build automation forms the building for continuous integration. The build should be coordinated across multiple platforms.

- **Allow for self-testing** – testing should also be automated. The purpose of continuous integration is to integrate the work done by different teams and to see if the application being built is functioning as expected.

- **Ensure staff commits to the project objectives** – developers should share their codes daily in order to ensure everybody is working towards a common goal. Regular integration of codes helps to ascertain that the project dependencies are recognized early so that the development team can work on them timely.

- **Faster builds** – builds that take longer to implement hinders application of continuous integration. Build made using modern tools are faster since it only builds changed files.

- **Testing in clone and the production-like environment** – it is risky to perform tests in environments that do not resemble the production system. It is important to test in a clone of the production environment. This is hard to achieve, since creating a clone of the production environment can be time-consuming.

- **Automate deployment** – continuous integration informs continuous delivery, which is the process of automating the deployment of software to test, testing the system, and the production environment.

Continuous Delivery (CD) – continuous integration and testing ensures that the project team provides constant progress updates.

This means that the teams will deliver their milestones continuously. It is at this stage that process automation is done in order to provide consistent results and deliver results that can be easily replicated and transferred as input for the next stage of development.

Continuous delivery is the most important part of the implementation of DevOps; that's why this stage comprises most of the tools in the DevOps methodology of software development.

Continuous delivery comprises taking the principles of continuous integration to the next stage. Once the software is built, at the end of the continuous integration stage, it will be delivered to the next phase in the software development lifecycle. After that, the application will be passed to the Quality Assurance team for quality checks and later to the operations team for final delivery to the production system. The primary objective of the CD is to get the features being delivered by the developers to the customer as soon as possible.

Continuous Testing – testing codes at every stage of the DevOps cycle is important since it ensures the code is fault free before sending it to the next stage of development. In a typical organization, Quality Assurance (QA) is the one responsible for this stage of software development. The specific processes used at this stage may vary depending on the nature of the project at hand and the customer's requirements as per the service level agreement.

Continuous testing is carried out by test and build automation systems. These systems are used to manage testing, workflow, and build processes by eliminating manual entry of configurations or settings. The systems are similar to the infrastructure as code systems that pass the tasks to the mainframe to handle. Traditionally, computers and compilers used to store programs in one source file. Nowadays, programs are complex and big, forcing the developers to split the files into many smaller source files that are stored in more than one source file. With the increasing number of source files to be compiled and executed, it became obligatory to automate the process of building and testing.

Today, build automation tools specify how software should be built and the specific dependencies required.

Continuous testing is achieved by checking all the aspects of an application and the environment. These aspects include user acceptance testing, security testing, application integration testing, integration testing, performance testing, functional testing, and unit testing. The biggest challenge in continuous testing is the absence of data sources required to perform some tests. Additionally, the cost implications may, at times, inhibit running tests on a continuous basis. In complex software development cycles, that are made up of many teams, the cost of designing test environments that will cater for all the teams may be very high.

To address this issue, test virtualization is applied. Here, virtual applications, services, and data sources are used. The virtual environment enables the test apps to test the software's functionality, integration, and performance without creating the real environment.

Continuous feedback and monitoring – feedback from clients can be collected in a number of ways, for example, by using tickets from customers, change requests from customers, complaints reported, ratings from in-app rating systems. The aim of continuous feedback is to confirm that the code created and integrated with the code received from other developers and with other components of the application is functioning as expected.

Recently many users prefer giving feedback through social media. Thus it's one of the avenues that the developers can utilize and can be incorporated in the design plans. The feedback mechanisms for DevOps should be agile in order to adapt to the rapid changes in the software market and also to adhere to policy changes.

Another way of getting feedback on the project progress is through monitoring. Monitoring data contains information that can be utilized for system optimization.

An efficient continuous monitoring system should be able to capture user opinions, software user behavior, system performance, and application performance. It is important for the operations team not just to gather this data but also analyze the data deeply.

Alerting is an important component that goes hand in hand with monitoring processes. Alerting is a feedback mechanism that helps the developer to find our potential issues before they affect the client. When selecting an alerting system, the developer should consider the following factors:

Impact – alerting systems will have different impacts depending on the system being designed. A big system spanning over multiple other systems or clients will have a bigger impact compared to one that affects a small subset of systems. Thus, the alerting system should be limited to incidents that have the most impact.

Urgency – not all issues are urgent. An urgent issue will require an immediate response or action. For example, a website going down such that clients cannot buy stuff means you are losing money and customers. This is an urgent issue compared to your blog site is down. Different organizations will categorize issues differently as being urgent, depending on their priority tasks. Thus it's important to consider all the stakeholders' input while designing an alerting system.

Target – this is the interested party, the persons that are affected by the alert. This can either be clients or a portion of clients or staff in the case of incidences internal to the organization. The target persons can sometimes be the people who are supposed to respond to the incident. For example, if an operational incident occurs, the systems should be able to alert the operations team only instead of notifying developers and QA teams at the same time.

Resources – while deciding on which alerting system to use, it is important to evaluate the resource available to respond to the particular incident. The developer should be able to establish whether the response team can cover all incident points and respond timely when an incident is reported. The response team should also be well facilitated to respond promptly, and they should be many in order to handle multiple incidents reported simultaneously.

Cost – like any other system, cost consideration is important in selecting an alerting system. The monitoring and alerting costs spans from the cost of monitoring service and its solutions to the storage space required to handle historical monitoring or alert data. The cost of sending our alerts should be factored in this, not forgetting the cost of responding to the incident.

Alerting is basically the process of generating events from the information that is collected from the monitoring tools. We will discuss more events in the next section.

System Events

Event management is a component of monitoring that deals with existing information around the impact on systems and services. For services that run in real-time, the tools will be required to capture the status of the components in real-time also. A monitoring system will be configured to monitor specific parameters or log based on a set event or signal if a threshold is passed or minimum conditions for alert have been met.

With the advancement in cloud computing, more software development activities are done on the web. Thus, developers would require an alert system on changes that may occur in the system when they are not in the office. In order to achieve this, automated alert systems will be implemented to notify the developers of system changes that may occur while they are away.

Alerting and monitoring systems nowadays have in-built ways of responding automatically to certain events. An example is the Nagios monitoring system, which can be customized for different alert circumstances. The handlers can perform various activities, from restarting services that crashed automatically to technical ticketing personnel to fix a hardware or software problem.

Automatic event handlers can reduce the amount of work the operations staff have to handle. But this is not risk-free. It is necessary to have the failure parameters clearly defined, and that the event handler process is understood well in order to be automated to avoid causing more problems during implementation.

An alert system cannot be 100% accurate all the time. Some times a false positive may occur when an event is created when actually there was no issue. False-positive events may call developers to action at the most inconvenient time only to find that it was not an issue to be attended to. On the other hand, you can receive a false negative event where an issue occurred, but the system failed to create an event for it, thus causing the technician to detect and resolve the issue late. There is a cost implication for both false positive and false negative events.

As time goes by, you will be required to tune up your monitoring and the alerting system as you understand the impact of reported issues and events. It is important to keep a log of the alerting system by collecting information on whether an action was taken for each reported event and the number of alerts that were actionable. Tracking trends in alert systems help in improving the effectiveness of alerts, as well as ensuring the responders are not inconvenienced with false events.

Assessing your tool environment

Before selecting a specific tool for your application, it is important to assess the state of the environment in which the tool will be implemented (ecosystem). A checklist can be applied to assess your tool environment. The first component to check before selecting a tool is whether the tool's function exists in your environment. In this section, we will explore the basic tools and the foundations that enable one to estimate the health of your environment.

When reviewing your environment to establish the best ecosystem for your tool, you will need to include information about who can access and use the tool. You should also provide data concerning multiple tools or tools whose functionalities overlap in your environment. This information will help to inform areas that require improvement or where training is required or whether a specific tool has to be replaced.

Aligning a tool with a process is important for tool usage. The excessive process leads to the increased cost to people as they try to maintain complicated frameworks around the processes. The fewer process often leads to a lack of team unity with the explosion of tools and methods of using tools.

Communication Tools

The selection of tool environments must start with communication. A good working environment is created from effective communication. Communication is the key to working in collaboration; the tools and process implemented by your company for interpersonal communication will obviously affect the organization's culture.

Many factors affect communication, which prevents finding a single communication tool that will meet all the needs of an organization. Thus it is important to examine a tool closely before making changes in the availability of that tool.

As a company grows, its communication needs change. For startups, simple chatting will suffice, but as the organization grows, emails become the best tool for communication. When employees are working in remote locations, video conference becomes the best tool for communication. In order to efficiently communicate using video, you will need to confirm that your team members have good headsets since the mic and speakers on laptops don't offer good quality sound and may discourage team members from interacting.

The selection of tools, platforms, or methods of communication is based on the content, urgency, context, and other factors of communication. Once these factors have been established, you can now look at other factors like the cost of the communication tool to be used. You can either use a paid version or a freeware version of the same tool.

Communication can make or break. Sometimes communication tools can be a distraction to project progress. Using the low-immediacy medium of communication like email for matters that need urgent response will cause problems of miss-communication.

Finally, when selecting a tool, it is important to strike a balance between cohesiveness and flexibility. If there are several communication tools or platforms, people will miss information since they will have to search for information needed in the many across all the platforms.

Tools and Technologies for the Implementation of DevOps

This section aims to examine the recent DevOps tools, how to select the right tool, and the steps taken by developers to improve the existing tools. IT processes usually use tools and templates to implement changes and create systems. The tools selected by developers in project delivery is very important since it affects the collaboration and communication between the developers, operators, and QA teams.

The waterfall methodology poses one challenge of focusing on discovering all parts of a tool strategy before implementing any single part. It is important to select a tool that will solve all the problems in the organization, deliver the innovation and software quickly, and at the same time, provide quality to the clients. It is important to note that there is no single tool that can deliver all these capabilities.

It is hard for developers to decide on the specific tools to use to implement DevOps for fear of selecting the wrong tool. Adopting tools that can help the developers visualize and track this dispute of time and lost efforts can assist in creating an environment that encourages continuous learning.

DevOps tools are the items that enable the developers to apply the principles of DevOps in the software development cycle. Some developers often underestimate the importance of DevOps tools stating that DevOps is not dependent on the tools. This section takes a critical look a DevOps toolset, how to optimize the tools, and how to select the right tools for your development environment. We will also explain outdated tools and how their continued use in your organization can affect the quality of the end product.

Why use Tools in DevOps?

Tools are an important component in any problem-solving endeavor. Developers and operators alike may be comfortable with a certain set of tools that they are used to. But this does not mean that they should not keep track of the latest development of the tools. Developers should be versatile by adopting new tools in order to increase the speed of delivery and efficiency of handling processes in the software development cycle.

Companies adopting infrastructure automation usually have a competitive advantage over those who have not adopted or are slow at adoption. While it is possible to manage servers manually, using a good configuration management tool will prove invaluable to an organization, especially in a dynamic development environment with high team turnover.

Additionally, a developer will find it hard to work on a system or environment without a version control tool in place. The efficiency of a system being designed can be compromised if the wrong tools are used. The success of an organization is based on the tools used in the implementation of DevOps principles.

Tools allow teams to collaborate more since software has evolved from being written by one person to being written by many people or teams from different locations. These team members must understand the codes developed by another team during the software development cycle and years after that. Thus, it is important to use a coordinated approach in selected and using tools on the project.

Tools are often confused with software programs. It is important to note that a tool can be hardware too. For example, choosing a hardware RAID solution over software RAID solution costs a little more but offers additional advantages like back up battery, and it's easier to maintain. The cloud services have led many developers to think of tools as software components only, neglecting the fact hardware can be a tool also.

Tool selection is important in the implementation of DevOps since not all tools are the same. Developers should be able to select the right tools based on the demand of the project. Some tools are good at collaboration while others are not, e.g., configuration management and source control tools.

Since DevOps is a cultural movement, tools will be used to enforce this culture. Thus, it is important to carefully select the tools that align properly with your organization's culture. Standardization of tools is important since technologies keep changing every day.

Components of DevOps Tools

Configuration management (CM) – configuration management dates back in the 50s when the US Department of Defense started it. Configuration management has been implemented in many sectors to date. CM is basically the procedure of creating and sustaining the consistency of a product's performance, its functional and physical attributes in the project life cycle. Configuration management encompasses the tools required to implement the system, policies, processes, and even documentation.

A good example of standards for configuration management in the software engineering industry is ITIL, IEEE, ISO, and SEI. Many a time people confuse infrastructure automation with configuration management.

Configuration management involves identification, maintenance of configuration, and verification of both software and hardware, such as patches and versions. It is simply managing the configuration of a system according to the requirement of the systems. For example, the code developed should be compatible with the Quality Assurance systems.

The benefits of including configuration management process in the DevOps approach include:

- It helps the developers in planning predictive and preventive maintenance.

- It facilitates tracking and resolving defects in the project.

- It enhances coordination between the development team and the operations team.

- It helps developers to circumvent configuration-related problems.

- Helps in the management of updates that are carried out simultaneously.

- Eliminates redundancy by ensuring consistency in the project delivery process.

- Configuration management helps to facilitate auditing, accounting, and verification of software systems.

- Using the configuration changes derived from configuration management, an organization can analyze the impact of the project at various stages of development (continuously).

Version Control – Version control is responsible for recording or tracking changes to files or sets of files stored within a system. The files can be source codes, assets, and documents concerning the software development project. Developers make changes in groups called commits or revisions. Every change and its metadata, like the user who made the changed and the time it was made, is stored in the software in accordance with the version control system. The version control systems can be distinguished from each other by the process by which the metadata and revision are stored. It can either be local, centralized, or a distributed version control system.

Local version control is accomplished by saving patch sets of changes in files on one node, which is local to where the files are stored, whereas a centralized version control is accomplished through one remote server that contained versioned files. Customers can check out the files from a centralized location. A distributed version control is accomplished through the entire repositories that are being replicated across diverse nodes.

Organizations should implement, train, utilize, and measure acceptance of tool usage of version control. This gives team members the capability of dealing with conflicts that ebb from having many developers working on the same project simultaneously and provide a safe mode to make changes and roll them back where necessary. The application of version control earlier in the project design cycle will help people adopt good habits.

When selecting the best tool in your ecosystem for source control management, you should search for one that encourages collaboration amongst team members.

Qualities that inspire collaboration include:

- Sharing the commit rights.

- Clearly defining processes for contributing.

- Curating contribution to personal repositories.

- Contributing to the repositories.

- Forking and opening repositories.

Some tools don't have collaborative features but have intrinsic system knowledge within your environment due to extended use. In such, collaboration can be applied, but it will be a bit tricky to apply.

There are several types of repository models that version control systems can take, either local, centralized, or distributed.

The local model has the repository located on the node that stores files. It is easy to set up, but it is the most vulnerable to system failure. For the client-server model, there is one central version of the repository in the server, and the developers work locally, make changes to the server in order to make the changes available to other developers. Since customers don't save the entire repository on a local machine, a centralized model is important for repositories that contain large binary files, where storing local versions of every version every file would be expensive for the client. In this case, the server is the one fault point.

A distributed version control system doesn't depend on a central server, every client that copies the repository will have a full copy of it, including its metadata. Most software projects are made of text files; thus, the overheads of storing large files are not expensive. Having a full local copy is advantageous since all actions can be carried out offline, thus allowing developers to work without an internet connection. This is important for teams that work remotely in areas without good internet coverage.

DevOps processes are highly repetitive, and thus developers use technology to help handle repetitive tasks by automating the processes. Automation helps the developers and operators to concentrate on the core business. Technology also helps in a great way to speed up some routine tasks, thus enabling an organization to deliver projects to their customers timely.

Technology helps in maintaining consistency of quality in processes or products designed. It also helps developers to easily re-use codes, tools, and design models in an efficient manner.

It is important to automate all routine processes, especially the testing processes, and set them up to achieve the speed and agility that the DevOps approach offers. Complex projects require sophisticated DevOps automation tools; the tools include:

- Infrastructure Automation tools

- Deployment Automation tools

- Configuration management tools

- Performance management tools

- Log management tools and

- Monitoring tools

We will discuss a few of the tools and how they can be implemented in the software design life cycle.

Infrastructure Automation Tools

This is a component of DevOps that allows businesses to easily scale and increase the speed with which the system can offer continuous delivery of feedback during the project's life cycle. An example of such systems is the cloud-based services like the AWS by Amazon. These tools do not require the developer to be physically present in the data center in order to access or/and configure the system.

Cloud-based services can be scaled up easily on-demand with little or no hardware costs incurred. An operator can remotely configure the servers to provide more space based on the traffic. All these processes can be easily automated since they are often repetitive.

Infrastructure automation is meant to reduce the load on developers of service management, thus increasing the quality, precision, and accuracy of the service to the client.

An example of infrastructure automation tools at work is the Convergence vs. congruence. Convergence is the procedure of arriving at an anticipated end result based on calculating the route from the starting point. If it fails, another run is executed to try to reach the goal by re-calculating the route by rolling back the changes and starting afresh. On the other hand, congruence involves starting from scratch with a blank slate and following a system of steps to achieve the desired state.

Infrastructure automation facilitates for definition control of how a system will be set up in the code, from system settings to the set of programs installed and running to the user management and configuration of the network.

Infrastructure as code (IaC) offers many benefits, including repeatability, consistency, easy documentation, and delivery of resilient processes that are fault-proof. This helps developers to free up time, improve the efficiency of codes and teams, and allows for flexibility in the system development cycle.

The advantages accrued from implementing Infrastructure as Code include:

- Updating system configuration is done faster by using the definition files and codes.

- Codes are not prone to errors, and the results can be replicated.

- IaC facilitates for thorough testing and deployment.

- Helps in the management of small changes, large infrastructure updates may contain errors that can be undetectable.

- It enables easy audit tracking and compliance using the definition files.

- It enables the developers to update multiple servers at the same time.

- It allows for longer system uptime with fewer breakdowns.

Provisioning automation is a component of infrastructure automation that allows companies to define infrastructure in clusters of dependent systems that are required to define their infrastructure as opposed to just single nodes. It is applied in the configuration of servers and then automatically using the configuration many times later. Provision automation tools can be used to install and set up infrastructure configuration.

Infrastructure automation tools can be categorized into three:

- **Application-centric tools** – these tools can manage both application servers and the applications running in the servers. These are special tools that comprise of libraries of automation tasks for supported technologies. These tools cannot be used for low-level tasks like the configuration of an Operation system's settings. The tools can be fully implemented in the automation of server-level tasks and application-level tasks.

- **Generic tools** – these are not technology-specific tools and can be programmed to handle any system development tasks be it the configuration of an Operating system or firewall ports settings. The problem with such tools is that they require a lot of work prior to using them as compared to application-centric tools. The advantage of such tools is that they can handle a wider range of tasks.

- **Deployment environment and deployment tools** – these are the DevOps tools that enable developers to achieve continuous integration and testing. The tools help developers to integrated process changes easily by identifying issues immediately a software is deployed. These tools can simultaneously deploy infrastructure configurations and application codes.

Examples of IaC tools in existence include SaltStack, Puppet, Cheff, CFEngine, and Ansible Tower.

Deployment Automation Tools

Specialized DevOps tools are required in order to manage automation of software deployment from one phase to the next. Deployment automation tools are the core of DevOps. The tools are used for tracking which version has been deployed and its node at any stage of the project life cycle.

Deployment automation tools manage the software components that are being deployed, its components and configurations that require updating, database components to be updated, and the configuration changes to the environment in which the components will be deployed.

An example of this is the application deployment process, which includes the planning, maintenance, and execution of the delivery of software release to the computed resources that are required.

Configuration Management Tools

These important DevOps tools help developers to achieve speed, scale, and consistent results in the project development cycle.

Complex routine tasks and configuration management is handled by this tool. With these tools, operators and developers will only be required to make changes on one server. It saves the developers the hustle of making changes in hundreds of servers repeatedly. Instead, a developer will enter the necessary changes in one place, and it will be automatically be replicated in all the available servers.

Performance Management Tools

These are DevOps tools that allow the developers or operators to receive real-time monitoring of project performance. The information gathered using this tool can be used in debugging the system in the event that an issue arises in the software development cycle.

Log Management Tools

Log management tools are DevOps tools that are used to solve design errors like aggregation, storage, and analysis of logs in a central location. Logging can be defined as the filtering, generating, analysis, and recording of processes that happen in a system. Before engaging on a task in a system, developers will first check the logs for any error message. Logs can keep system error message that dates back many years. This can help designers and developers alike to resolve current issues based on experiences logged in the past. A system can generate hundreds of logs in a minute. On systems running on multiple servers, the number of logs created can be overwhelming. This is why the DevOps approach uses tools that can manage the logs by simply reading through the error messages in the bulk of log files.

Monitoring Tools

Monitoring is a key element of DevOps. It's important for all stakeholders to be updated timely on the progress of the project. These tools ensure that teams are notified when changes occur in design infrastructure and related services. An example of monitoring tools is called Nagios, which assists DevOps teams in identifying and rectifying design problems identified.

Monitoring in a broad component of DevOps. Monitoring activities involve collecting logs and metrics. In monitoring, the tools collect various server metrics like downtime, memory and processor utilization, disk performance, among others. One can also monitor the queuing of data to be entered into a database.

Application of configuration management helps developers to set up monitoring of new systems. It is important to set the right parameters for monitoring to avoid instances where a fault occurs, and you realize the monitoring system was down. New deployments can be configured to allow for monitoring of important system parameters. Configuration management systems have monitoring capabilities in-built to provide real-time information on system performance.

With the coming of the internet and interconnections of systems, the security of the system has become a major concern of IT departments. It is important for designers to perform security checks regularly to ensure the system is safe from remote invasion. In this case, developers will tack failed login attempts, and they will also set up detection systems to keep track of any invasive activities to the system.

Monitoring in DevOps should be carried out at all stages of the software development life cycle; it helps to keep track of the state of the system and ensure that the system meets the predefined conditions. Monitoring and testing are DevOps processes that are closely related and work interchangeably to ensure delivery of quality products to the customers hence increasing companies' competitive advantage.

Management of Hardware Lifecycle

Organizations will handle hardware lifecycle management in their lifetime. However, cloud services have greatly reduced the occurrence of such. The hardware life cycle starts with planning and acquiring or leasing, then installation, followed by maintenance and repair, and ends with returning or recycling hardware that has outlived its usefulness.

Provision automation tools can be used to reduce the number of manual tasks that must be carried out during installation of the hardware and during maintenance after installation. Without this, the system admin will have to repeat installation procedures in each system, which is prone to errors. Decommissioning procedures can also be automated as well in order to free the developer and allow him or her time to concentrate on core activities.

Output (artifact) Management

An artifact is an output from any step in the software development cycle. Dependent on the programming language, the output can be different things, for example, libraries, assets to applications. Output repository should be:

- Safe

- Trustworthy

- Very stable

- Easy to access

- Can be versioned

Maintaining a repository of artifact allows the developer to treat dependencies statistically. The common versioned library can be stored as an artifact separately from software version control hence allowing all teams to use the exact same shared library. Binaries are built only once. This assists in eliminating complexities by ensuring the same binary are used throughout the test cycles and promotion in between builds.

Artifact repositories allow the developer to store the artifacts in the manner that they appear. Some repository stores only one version of the package at a time. It is tricky to describe the history of such repositories. Also, it increases the duplication factor of package storage to maintain a separate output repository depending on the environment in your workflow.

For open sources operating systems like Ubuntu and CentOS, the package manager uses external package repositories. This tends to be unstable. When systems are down, problems with systems at the remote package store can lead to building issues if the system is dependent on external resources availability.

More software dependencies and application sellers rely on downloading software from external providers. You need to evaluate your risks and how to migrate your identified risks. Most people trust external providers since the software provided works, and other people are using it.

Version control can be used to store binaries despite it not being the right use of resources. Developers will not modify binaries directly, thus cloning a repository with many binaries will affect the bandwidth and build time.

The table below shows types of artifacts and the purpose:

Type	Purpose
Zip files, tarball	General
DLLs	Windows
gem	Ruby
Jar, War	Java
Deb, rpm	Linux

Figure 4: Types of artifacts and their purpose

However small, the need to pass security compliance requirements doesn't exist in your environment. But as the project and organization grow in complexity, this may be a requirement. Possession of a dedicated local artifact repository will facilitate for smooth changeover to these requirements.

The local development environment has the same access to the internal artifact repository as the other build and deploys mechanisms in the development environment. This reduces the chances of it not working on other platforms or remote platforms since the same packages and dependencies used in production are used in the local development setting. When access is blocked, this resistance can lead to new ways of handling things that evade security. In case you don't have internet access in your ecosystem, you will have to host your own space. To do this, you will require software repositories, ruby servers, dependency management, among others. Many shared services will have to be replicated.

Management of Infrastructure

Infrastructure management is beyond the scope of the basics of a robust tool ecosystem in your environment as it is only part of recognizing the resources needed, and the functions they have within the development environment. These elements are the fundamentals of any organization's wellbeing from using email as the communication gateway amongst the internal and external clients to the website that updates and teach about your product and services.

Sometimes Information Technology can be perceived as a cost-intensive department resulting in underfunding of the department. In small to mid-size companies, one person can decide on the tools that will be used by the company to implement the DevOps methodology. This can overwhelm a person since he or she will be responsible for ensuring the methodology works and that he or she addresses all the bottlenecks that may occur during implementation. He will also be charged with the responsibility of ensuring that the chosen systems operate optimally.

It is preferable to provide elements of the infrastructure through code, where the code is handled like other software, data should be recovered from back-ups, use code repository, and computer system resources. As discussed earlier, this is referred to as infrastructure automation. Here, before the code is sent to production, it is handled like the base software. The code will be developed on a common local development environment and versioned using the version control.

How the system is set up and described will be defined by the infrastructure automation. This will span from the settings of the systems to the user management software. Infrastructure automation allows for handling repeatable, highly consistent, documentable, and resilient processes that can handle failure.

Automation helps free time for developers, increases the efficiency of team members, and enables flexibility and ability to estimate foreseen risks. Additionally, it increases the confidence levels of staff in handling the processes and deployment, thus reducing time wasted in solving errors created by systems variations.

When humans handle repetitive tasks, they are bound to make mistakes. Manual set up of the system is prone to errors of omission by the operator, whereby the system is configured inconsistently since a change is the processes omitted on an older system or the person misses a step on the checklist of manual steps. Computers handle repetitive tasks better and more accurate than humans do. Implementing an automation code is a step toward disaster recovery. When a developer deploys a system, knowledge is generated, creating a Single Point of Knowledge (SPOK).

Creating a common method of describing infrastructure in code amongst your team by having infrastructure as a code system will tremendously minimize the number of 'distinct snow-flake' servers in existence. People usually fear to handle servers that were configured manually because they fear to temper with the settings that were made to get them running. Automation leads to an increased server to people ration since the time required to set up each server is less.

Infrastructure automation makes it easy for system administrators to comprehend and perform machine set up necessary to accomplish their specific tasks. Infrastructure as code system enables developers and other stakeholders to understand the system better.

Infrastructure as a code is advantageous for implementing DevOps; thus, it is the first option for software designers. DevOps tools are better understood when they are in use in the software development cycle. Since DevOps is a culture, the efficiency and impact of a tool will be affected by the organization's culture or level of adoption of DevOps methodology.

The choice of infrastructure to adopt depends on your specific needs. Automation is important for organizations of any size, from start-ups to established organizations. An organization should invest in human resources or people that have a good understanding of both manual configuration and automated systems. Versatility in the software design industry is key to continuous improvement.

As businesses expand, they become complex by requiring extra resources, employees, services, and applications. As more people interact with these resources, it creates more interesting boundaries and edge cases. As an organization matures from a startup into a fully-fledged company and adopts its own automation standards, the need to manage its infrastructure becomes critical.

As the company grows, it must consider the following:

- **Manage system configuration drift** – configuration drift is the case where the servers will change or drift away from the usual configuration occasionally. Configuration drift can be caused by manual settings, updates on the server, and errors. It is in order to prevent the occurrence of such drifts. This can be done by maintaining an individual node to regularly check the desired settings against the actual settings on the server and automate the self-correcting processes for any inconsistency found.

- **Completely avoid manual server settings** – also called snowflake server. This is a server that has its current settings entered manually using the command line, config files, manually applied patches, and sometimes even Graphic User Interface (GUI) settings and installations. It is difficult to manage such a system in case of failure since the developer will have to track the manual settings' checklist. Infrastructure automation can be adopted to avoid manual settings of systems. Another way of handling this is by entering configuration in smaller batches. This is achieved by setting up one system at a time slowly until the settings can be utilized in recreating the server from scratch in its desired configuration.

- **Using versioned and artifacts infrastructure code** – an appropriated infrastructure automation solution is one with a version control system and an artifact repository. This enables the code that describes the server configuration to be versioned hence enjoying the advantages of versioning, for instance, being able to roll back changes to the last good version effortlessly or to have post-commit hooks running a test against the infrastructure code. This approach embraces the DevOps methodology since all team members will contribute to refining the infrastructure code to align it with the design processes.

- **Should maximized complexity** – by specifying the version of configuration in each platform type or version, infrastructure automation tools will allow developers to manage diverse environments with minimum costs irrespective of their job description or titles.

Advanced DevOps Tools Concepts

Basic DevOps tools are so indispensable; it is difficult to work efficiently without these tools. Working without infrastructure automation results in an enormous number of tasks for the operations team, for example, avoiding, scrutinizing for, and mitigating configuration drift and snowflake servers. Development tasks minus version control is risky, especially when the job gets lost, and wrong changes go online, forcing the developers to roll back configurations. At this stage, communication is key since the operations and development teams need to work together to achieve this.

Advanced tools can also be employed in the process of generating, deploying, and running software. The development team can work without these advance tools if they choose to. But it is important to discuss them since incorporating them in the software development cycle can help increase the quality and efficiency of the final product.

The advanced tools include:

Sandbox automation – this is a sandbox testing ecosystem or environment which allows the developer to test code changes and carry out an experiment using varying infrastructure elements without affecting production. The processes involve capturing the definition of the sandbox so that the developer can easily and quickly reproduce or share the provisions that constitute a sandbox. An example is the Test Kitchen, which is sandbox automation that is able to run on laptops and is compatible with several cloud platforms and other virtualization technologies like Amazon EC2, Digital ocean, Openstack, and Dockers. The test kitchen is a static configuration that can utilize version control in software development.

Planning and task visualization – a key foundation of Lean manufacturing, as discussed earlier in chapter 1, is the just in time (JIT) manufacture as a way of limiting the production of parts to only what was required at that time. This reduces waste by not having excesses of materials being generated and lying around uselessly.

This approach helps to modernize the entire manufacturing process. Minimizing the amount of work in progress to a practicable amount is the core of lean manufacturing, which helps to ensure that the teams don't take on more tasks than they can practically handle within a set period of time.

Companies use ticketing or bug-tracking systems to keep track of tasks currently being done and to plan for future tasks. A good system will have some visualization tools for representing tasks like the Gantt chart. Visualization tools provide means of automatically restraining the size of tasks (workload) by allowing a specified number of tasks to be designated as work in progress (WIP). Team members will use this approach to limit the amount of workload in their respective inboxes. Automation of this is essential for teams instead of having them remember the tasks in progress all the time.

The ability to switch tasks from one team to the other is very important in the software development cycle. It encourages the teams to work collaboratively, especially when the tool allows for smooth communication or feedback on why a particular process is being carried out. Allowing different teams to see the progress of their counterparts encourages collaboration and avoids duplication of tasks.

Deployment – this was always a cause for disagreement in the past when software development team members that wrote the code were siloed off from the system admins who deployed and maintained the code. Initially, deployment would involve a system admin taking the code, via a physical media, to a server or workstation and installing it. This was a very slow and awkward procedure, which is prone to errors, typical of manual procedures.

Present-day deployment tools come in a diversity of forms nowadays, but all geared towards automating the development processes as much as possible reduce the time spent by developers and also to reduce errors.

The deployment process will apparently vary depending on the kind of software that is being deployed. Software codes that run in other hardware systems like printers and televisions will be deployed differently than mobile software, so will the deployment of a website. The key elements of an efficient deployment system are:

- Should have clear steps. To begin setting up a deployment system, the developer will be required to specify all the necessary steps required for deployment. It is common knowledge that you cannot automate a process that you cannot fully and easily define. Once the steps to follow have been clarified, it is easy to start the automating pieces of the processes. Developers should ensure each step is documented so as to share the knowledge of the processes with new employees easily, stakeholders as well as aid in troubleshooting if anything goes wrong.

- The system should have a number of error checking and error handling mechanisms. Deployment is a very sensitive stage in the project development cycle. It is important to implement a system that will capture errors prior to presenting them to the client. An ideal deployment tool will check for possible errors at every stage and make those errors visible to the first responders for action. The system should be able to back out and stop deployment in case an error occurs. This is necessary in order to prevent the error from being entrenched in the final production.

- A good deployment system should have minimal overhead. A lengthy and tedious deployment process will require the developers to deploy less frequently; hence, it is likely to have issues. Whereas it is possible to automate the entire deployment process, it is not advisable to do so. It is advisable that most of the deployment processes should be carried out with human intervention. This will minimize overhead and will be less costly in the long term.

Selecting DevOps Tools

Not all tools are suitable for all technologies. And one single tool cannot be applied in implementing different types of activities. For example, when a developer is using the Java programming language to design a system, he will definitely use the JUnit tool, alternatively for a developer using the Microsoft technologies will use the NUnit tool in his project.

Although there are tools that support multi-programming languages, for example, Cucumber and Jerkins, there are a number of tools currently to choose from when implementing DevOps.

Several factors can be used in selecting DevOps tools. These factors are common for all types of tools that you will adopt in your environment. Common factors include:

- **Development of the product** – a dynamic software will be quicker to get new features and to support new operating systems and platforms and will easily handle any security vulnerabilities.

- **The health of the teams** – Active team members will be beneficial in adopting tools. For example, in open source software, the developers will not reinvent the wheel, all they do is to learn how others handled the problem at hand and use the lessons to create or improve existing systems. An open-source solution with a large team working on it will be more efficient.

- **Whether the tools can be customized locally or in-house** – a tool that can be customized to fit the developers' needs is good to both the technological and human aspects of the environment. This is essential in complex projects that have many people working on the development cycle. Such a tool will be improved over time such that it will part of the organization and will make the work of the developers and operators easier.

It is important to consider the capabilities and compatibility of tools before settling for one to use in the software development project. The tools of choice will probably be based on its functions and the expected outcome. For instance, managing the source code can be an intended outcome, so the developer will categorize all the source code repositories under a single container then select the best tool to handle the repositories. Examples of source code repositories include Git, Apache subversion and mercurial.

Chapter Four

DevOps and Cloud Computing

In this chapter, we will explore more on how cloud computing can enhance the adoption of DevOps in various organizations. We will also delve into the deployment of full-stack and various cloud services models that can be adopted in DevOps. You will learn how cloud computing can facilitate DevOps.

DevOps and cloud computing can be used interchangeably to support each other. DevOps tasks can be carried out in the cloud while at the same time, the DevOps process can be handled from the cloud. Cloud services offer flexibility, agility, and resilience that is required for handling DevOps processes. Cloud-based processes minimize the challenges related to the development environment from the testing phase to the product delivery stage. Many businesses seek to use cloud services to reduce the costs incurred in development and testing environments.

In this chapter, we will study models of cloud computing for DevOps and analyze the value proposition of DevOps as a capability on the cloud.

Cloud as a Facilitator for DevOps

The main objective of DevOps is to minimize challenges that can be met by developers and operators in the project's life cycle. This increases the efficiency of the project design process. DevOps requires that the developer work on an environment that resembles the environment in which the product will be deployed.

As systems and processes become complex, the need for storage and remote handling increases. The cloud offers an efficient way of handling these processes and holding a large volume of data generated in a cost-effective manner. The advantages of implementing projects on the cloud over traditional platforms include:

- Cloud platform offers higher value – when an organization migrates some of its processes to the cloud, it relieves the internal physical resources, which will be dedicated to other important activities of higher value.

- Cloud services allow for pay as you go – this means that the organization only pays for what it needs and when it needs it. Also, by so doing, the organization will not have to worry itself with the support software required like anti-virus, email services, security software, etc. which will be provided and maintained by the cloud service provider.

- Cloud services are quick to set up – cloud services are easily scalable and easy to set up. It is relatively quick to deploy an application on the cloud compared to using internal resources.

- Cloud offers a dynamic load pattern and flexible scalability – the cloud can handle tasks/loads of varying magnitude without requiring updates or upgrades of infrastructure. Thus, the organization can offload the heavy task to the cloud without worrying much about the components that handle the tasks.

One of the goals of developers is to test the systems in a production environment. Production like environments may not be available for developers at the project design stage hence posing quality issues in the project design cycle. Cloud computing is used to address this challenge during software development in the following ways:

- Cloud computing offers faster environment provisioning, which provides developers with any environment of their demand.

- The cloud provides developers with a dynamic environment. A dynamic test environment is cheaper to implement and manage compared to a static test environment.

- Cloud allows the developers to create an environment that fits the specific test of the process he would wish to run.

- Cloud services can quickly and easily be configured to match the needs of developers.

- Service virtualization technologies operating in the cloud platform enables the developers to simulate specific services required for testing without having to provide real-time instances of the services.

Implementing DevOps on environments hosted on cloud servers enables the developers to securely test the software in a production-like environment at a very low cost.

Cloud Deployment

In order to deploy a cloud application, the cloud environment must be configured to handle the application. A combination of deployment and configuration in the cloud is referred to as full-stack deployment.

An organization can use full-stack deployment in cases where the environment and related apps are provisioned as one unit that can be deployed. Such systems require little or no changes and updates on the existing environment.

Which is the Right Cloud Model for DevOps?

When choosing a cloud service, the developer must first specify the scope of tasks that he/she would wish was handled on the cloud and the amount that will be handled locally. To achieve this, two popular service models for cloud computing are used:

- Infrastructure as service (IaaS) and

- Platform as a Service (Paas).

Infrastructure as a Service (IaaS)

When implementing cloud computing using the IaaS model, cloud systems will manage the underlying infrastructure and provide the developer with services for virtualized infrastructure. The user will then handle the installation, data and application, patching, and management of the operating system.

Implementation of DevOps is dependent on the cloud service model selected by the developer. In the IaaS model, the developer's organization will manage the entire design cycle. The developer should acquire the right tools and ensure proper integration to form the delivery channel. The organization will be responsible for the collaboration between the development and operations teams as per DevOps culture. Even with the cloud services, there is a need to eliminate silos that often occur between the development team delivering the code and the operations teams that delivers the infrastructure that's hosted on the cloud.

The cloud helps greatly by offering the IaaS to the teams in charge of application delivery, but even with this, there still is a need to apply the right DevOps tools in order to achieve the full potential of the DevOps methodology.

Platform as a Service (PaaS) Cloud Model

In this model, the user only handles the application and data while the rest of the services are handled by the cloud platform. In this model, the application development and tools for testing will be made available as services on the cloud platform, which can be accessed by the developers. Since the cloud handles most of the required services, the development teams will, therefore, concentrate on the rapid delivery of applications. An example of a system using the PaaS model is the Bluemix by IBM, which hosts a set of tools that provide all the services required by developers to implement DevOps. In this model, the delivery team will just use the applications on the platform without caring much about how they are presented to them.

DevOps services available in the PaaS model include the following:

- Web-based Integrated Development Environment (IDE) services

- Monitoring and analytics services

- Deployment services.

- Security scanning and testing services

- Task management and Planning services

- Building and development as service

PaaS cloud model offers a scalable runtime environment for apps that run in dissimilar environments in the project's life cycle (starting from the development stage to testing up to the production and implementation stage).

Application of DevOps on Hybrid Cloud Services

Hybrid cloud is a popular technology in cloud computing. Physical infrastructure and cloud represent a popular cloud scenario commonly applied in cloud computing. This is commonly used as the default scenario in cloud platforms. An example of this is the mainframe apps and systems that handle heavy data for record apps that will not be migrated to the cloud because of technology or cost implications. During the migration of project workload to the cloud, there will be an extended period of time when the physical and cloud structure will coexist.

Another scenario for hybrid cloud services is the on-premise and off-premise cloud. Here, the organization will implement an off-premise cloud (public) for some applications and an on-premise (private) cloud for other applications. Many companies prefer to maintain a low-cost off-premise cloud to cater to its development environments while at the same time, maintain an on-premise cloud for its data center to handle production tasks.

Hybrid cloud services also consist of IaaS and PaaS models when a customer prefers to handle new applications using PaaS while at the same time, implement IaaS for record tasks.

Examples of hybrid cloud environment include:

- When a company uses a public cloud for software development, testing, and other non-production processes, while at the same time implements an on-premise cloud to handle production processes.

- When a business requires portable application tasks in multiple cloud services so as to ensure the client lock-in does not exist or to provide the capability for deploying critical tasks in multiple cloud service providers.

- When an organization controls a public PaaS for experimenting with new applications and would want to migrate them to a private cloud service once the experiment is successful.

- Where a company has a system of engagement apps deployed in a cloud environment, and the system of record apps for backend services still exist in on physical infrastructure like the mainframe computer.

The essential obligation for implementing DevOps with a hybrid cloud approach is the needed prerequisite for the deployment of applications across many cloud platforms and physical settings. An example of such a system deployed using the hybrid cloud approach is the UrbanCode by IBM; it has patterns that use application designs to map apps and configurations to multiple environments, both physical and cloud. This allows for automated apps to be deployed across complex hybrid environments.

Chapter Five

How DevOps Handles Recent Technology Challenges

In this chapter, we will discuss how DevOps has been able to solve recent IT challenges. For instance, how DevOps can be used in the development of mobile Apps. We will also explore the ALM processes, agile in the project cycle, how to manage multiple-tier apps. Furthermore, we will explore how DevOps can be applied to an enterprise business and supply chains. Recently, all over the world, the Internet of Things (IoT) is largely being adopted in the development of Artificially Intelligent systems. We will explore how DevOps helps developers and operators navigate the Internet of Things (IoT).

DevOps was popularized by web-based companies like Etsy, Netflix, and Flickr. These companies implemented DevOps in solving large scale IT projects. In this chapter, you will study the challenges that businesses face nowadays and how DevOps can be adopted to address these challenges.

Mobile Technology

In the current world, mobile applications (apps) have become a ubiquitous part of many businesses. Mobile apps are a more efficient way of collecting or presenting information to clients. Mobile apps can be used for facilitating transactions or to process employee information in the portal. Mobile apps are an example of complex systems that will require a combination of various services to produce a functional app.

Adoption of DevOps requires that the mobile-app teams of developers are brought on-board first together with other software development teams. Mobile Apps are usually deployed in apps stores popularly known as play store for Android devices. These are vendor-managed environments that assist in the deployment of the apps. Apple devices use the App store to deploy apps. Apple devices are usually locked, such that you cannot install apps directly to the phone without going through the App Store.

Corporate data usually resides in the mainframe servers. Allowing clients to access information on your main servers can be beneficial. But to achieve this requires a lot of security checks and design considerations so that the client gets just what is relevant to him or her. Delivering apps to the client can be hindered by skill gap, siloed departments, and numerous platforms that course delays in release cycles.

In order to timely and efficiently release mobile apps to the clients, many organizations are adopting DevOps approach that is centered on the speed of delivery and efficiency at a relatively lower cost and without compromising on the stability and quality of the apps. Customers generally require their apps to be designed and released in the shortest time possible, DevOps offers just that. Application of DevOps concepts and principles in mobile app development is an inevitable procedure for designers of new mobile technology-related apps.

The Application Life Cycle Management Processes (ALM)

As mentioned earlier in the book, ALM is basically a group of processes implemented to manage the life of an app as it's designed from an idea to an app that can be deployed in a relevant platform for maintenance. ALM forms the concept behind the DevOps process for the design and maintenance of mobile apps. DevOps offers ALM a wider scope by including business proprietors, operations, and clients as part of the process.

Application of Lean and Agile

DevOps methodology utilized the lean and agile concepts in its implementation. As a result, it reduces the wastage of resources in the project implementation cycle. Automation is applied in handling repetitive tasks, thus reducing the development time for apps. Automation also helps team members to be innovative and responsive since they spend less time in developing tools, the simply re-use existing tools.

Lean manufacturing is aimed at improving both the continuous improvement of the final product and at the same time, reduce waste in the entire manufacturing process. Agile methodology came into existence in 2001 when a group of 17 people, including Alistair Cockburn and Martin Fowler, developed the Agile Manifesto. This was meant to improve on the tenets of the waterfall model.

The agile approach was further improved with development approaches such as Extreme Programming (XP), scrum, and SAFe. Thus, Agile was the core driver for DevOps. Agile enabled developers to code faster than before, but this also required the testers to test the codes at supersonic speeds and deploy to Dev and test servers even faster and eventually to production. The operations team could not handle the speeds of developers. This called for better coordination between the developers and operations teams.

The agile approach seemed to improve the efficiency of the development processes, only thus creating a backlog at the operations stage. The developers could develop codes faster than the operators could test. DevOps approach came in to reduce cycle time from project inception to the time the product is delivered to the customer. Here continuous integration, which is a core principle of agile and continuous delivery, was brought forth by DevOps to address the challenge.

DevOps projects are characteristically based on the Agile framework, for efficient and rapid turnaround of the development and software implementation cycle. The outdated waterfall model cannot keep up with the advantages that agile and DevOps brings on board. Agile methodologies' success is based on the following core objectives:

- Change adoption is most preferred as opposed to adherence to project plans.

- Collaboration with the client is emphasized more compared to contract negotiation.

- Functional software is move valued as opposed to intensive documentation.

- Communication amongst the team is more valued as opposed to the processes and tools.

- There are many benefits accrued from implementing principles of Agile in software development; these include:

- Agile practices help teams to maximize productivity since the operations are lean.

- Agile enables team members to organize themselves and focus on the project objectives, requirements, and design.

- Agile practices promote continuous attention to technical improvement and excellence hence developing quality designs.

- It promotes effective communication hence resulting in the delivery of high-quality products.

- It promotes collaboration between the developers and testers; thus, bugs are identified and resolved faster.

- The agile culture brings forth motivated staff that can be trusted and can collaboratively develop quality products.

- Enhances the quick and continuous delivery of products.

- The agile cycle accepts and processes change requests at any stage of the development.

Application of lean and agile principles in the App development team and stakeholders across the entire project life cycle is the key concept for the DevOps approach. Agile can be scaled to handle new challenges using different frameworks like the Scaled Agile Framework (SAFe) and Disciplined Agile Delivery (DAD).

In some enterprises, scrum has been seen to help in scaling agile to large teams of developers. These frameworks help in the implementation of agile at the enterprise level. Whichever framework is used to scale agile, the basic principles of agile are used and applied best practices to support them in achieving efficient and effective apps.

Multiple Layers (tier) Applications

Due to the complexity of the latest Apps and the demand for advanced features, applications designed will most like extend many platforms. Each platform will have its own unique tools, change processes, and skill requirements. Multi-layer systems integrate apps, desktop, web, and mobile apps on both the front and back end systems such as packaged apps, the application running on mainframe servers, and data storage systems.

Handling the parts of multiple-layer systems hosted on different platforms is not an easy task even for experienced developers. It is, therefore, necessary to automate the build processes at every stage of the project life cycle. In order to provide business value, the developers should adopt consistent deployment practices, which will help ensure that the teams are utilizing reliable and replicable processes.

DevOps in Business Enterprises

Businesses today rely on the speed of Information Technology to deliver applications. Many organizations and businesses operate packaged apps that are deployed on local computers. These systems pose challenges like:

- Unfavorable regulatory policies.

- Use of complicated processes.

- Developer's skills gaps

- Developers working in silos.

- Delays in app releases and wastage of resources.

DevOps can be implemented in businesses to facilitated planning, development, and continuous testing to ensure the cycle is done efficiently. Nowadays, apps are cross-platform and thus need for a sequential approach in their development. This is where DevOps comes in to allow apps to be developed tested and delivered in high quality, faster, and reduce the cost incurred to develop the software. Application of DevOps in system development gives the organization a competitive advantage.

Software Supply Chain

A software supply chain is a new concept that is slowly catching up in the software development scene. A supply chain is a system of businesses, technologies, information, and resources used in conveying a product or service from one supplier to the other and eventually to the final consumer. The suppliers in the chain may be internal or external to the organization.

Implementation of DevOps in organizations using the supply chain model is challenging since the associations among the suppliers are handled using contracts and Service Level Agreements (SLA) as opposed to collaboration and communication that is proposed by DevOps. Despite this challenge, DevOps can still be applied in such organizations by sharing the processes with the suppliers. The difference here will be that, in the delivery pipeline, each supplier will own different stages of the pipeline. It is important in this case for developers and suppliers to use a common set of tools, and a shared asset source is needed.

Additionally, a task management tool can be used to report on all tasks being worked on by the suppliers. Using a common asset source provides the mechanism for transferring assets over the pipeline for continuous delivery.

DevOps in the Internet of Things (IoT)

In the beginning, the data that was shared on the internet was generated by people. Recently, devices connect to the internet to transmit more data than people do. When devices are interconnected, they form a network of devices called the Internet of Things (IoT).

DevOps is an important approach for such devices because of the co-dependence of hardware and the corresponding software that runs on it. The devices are designed and created using continuous engineering methodology. This methodology utilizes DevOps to ensure the software running the devices is of high quality and has the right engineering specs.

In continuous engineering, the operators are the hardware and systems engineers who design and create hardware for the IoT devices. In this case, the software and hardware development will follow totally different development cycles. Thus, there is a need for the application of DevOps principles to ensure that there is close collaboration between the developers, testers, and the system engineers working on the project cycle.

The delivery of the software and hardware components must be well-coordinated in order to deliver quality systems. Other principles of DevOps, like continuous delivery and testing, remain the same. In continuous engineering, the simulation will be used to test the compatibility of the hardware and the developed software during development.

Chapter Six

Working with DevOps: A Case Study of IBM

This chapter will discuss the best DevOps practices implemented by executive companies. Our case study organization is IBM. We will learn how IBM applies principles of DevOps in designing and implementing its IT products. We will learn how IBM organizes its team and how you can organize your IT teams using a similar approach. In this chapter, we will also identify the goals of DevOps and how DevOps transformation has taken place. Finally, we will be able to derive lessons from DevOps end results.

International Business Machine (IBM) is among the pioneer companies in the implementation of DevOps across all departments in the company. At IBM, DevOps was pioneered at IBM's Software Group (SWG) and is currently applied in all divisions in IBM. In this chapter, we will learn how DevOps capabilities were used in the implementation of IBM SWG. This was done by IBM's Rational Collaborative Life Cycle Product management team.

SWG is a unique product from IBM since it was designed as an open-source software. The delivery team posted all its codes and the work in progress, including all detailed work items on the website www.jazz.net. The website is available for the public; a registered member can look at the work plans, on-going tasks, and the log of all past development tasks accomplished during the development of the software.

Role of Management in DevOps Implementation

DevOps is a culture, a movement that a company can adopt in order to deliver software development projects quickly. In many organizations, culture is a quality that is hidden, cannot be seen. But its impact is clearly visible. Culture signifies the values and behaviors in an organization from the top management down to the employees.

It is impossible to understand the companies' culture until you go onboard on significant change. Pessimistic people will sit back and watch to see if it is only a passing whim. It is at this point that leaders are identified. It is important to create an approach to enable you to understand the dynamics of culture and to know who is who so as to handle the actual inhibitors of progress.

To manage the dynamic nature of culture, the IBM SEG management team used the following approaches:

- **Selecting the right leaders:** the main role of a leader is to ensure the team is working towards the same goal. A leader should enable the team to have a common understanding of the project inhibitors, project objectives, changes in processes, and they should all have a common starting point.

- **Stakeholder engagement** – leaders must support the changes in the project, management, and employees across diverse development disciplines. The management should bring together enterprise stakeholders, project architects, system developers, software testers, and operators working on the project.

- **Track improvements and outcomes** – it is important to have a set of vital parameters that integrates both the required efficiencies and the outcome of the business. The goals and parameters should set the bar high and hold developers accountable, but care should be taken so that they don't cause disengagement of teams.

- **Set the ball rolling with initial successes** – leaders should be able to understand the inefficiencies that can occur in a project and use the set parameters for measuring improvements in the areas to set the momentum for change.

- **Communicate efficiently and listen to their subjects** – a good leader should understand the dynamics of the proposed change is affecting the team. A leader should have regular one on one sessions with the technical teams, the management teams and process leaders in order to know the buy-in of the team, their perspectives on the bottlenecks and identify any opportunities for the leaders to share their view on project priorities and the software development project progress. A leader should be available for his or her team to advise and help to eliminate impediments they may face in attaining the project's objectives. Effective communication from the leader will motivate the team to work towards the same goal.

Team Formation

IBM has been keen on the implementation of DevOps for many years. Its software development team, called IBM SWG Rational Collaborative Life Cycle Management product team, is one of the teams that developed over 70 software development tools under software delivery planning, apps deployment, analytics, apps monitoring, management of software quality, and software development.

The SWG product team from IBM is comprised of four teams working in over 25 locations in about 10 countries globally. Prior to the implementation of DevOps, the SWG team worked on an annual release schedule, which included six months of lead time in determining the components that should fall in the yearly release plans.

Setting DevOps Goals

There was a feeling from the SWG team that they usually delayed in responding to changes in the market as well as changes in demand from clients. The team purposefully decided that they need to shorten the actual project delivery time all the way from the development and test phases, including the collaboration and communication with the enterprise stakeholders and clients. To help the team achieve this, the goal was adjusted from annual releases to quarterly releases.

Moreover, the team required to fast-track its development to deliver new features more often, the team had to move quickly to provision for cloud delivery models, mobile development, testing mobile, and other functionalities to address the shift in technology. The SWG crew finally chose to implement DevOps principles and practices to change the manner in which the crew develops software to deliver quality products to its clients in a timely and more frequent manner.

To achieve this change in the scope required for a change in the overall culture of IBM, teams of four workgroups were formed, which were made up of representatives from the management team and the technical department leaders. The workgroup studied the existing software delivery process from start to end and was tasked to change the way the processes were handled.

The working group came up with measures and actions to address the key issues in the software development cycle. As a result, a continuous delivery team was established, which included a clergyman who taught the team about best practices across the organization.

To kick-start the process of adoption of DevOps, the IBM SWG crew identified three goals, namely:

I.   To develop a culture of continuous improvement.

II.   Utilize tools in a manner that will ensure consistency, scalability to other teams, and create easy to trace capabilities.

III.   Restructure the processes and adopt new practices.

Lessons Learned from the Adoption of DevOps

This section describes the lessons learned and steps taken by the SWG team from the implementation of DevOps:

Intensifying agile practices – the existing agile practices in IBM were intensified to cover a wider scope, including clients, enterprise stakeholders, and operations teams, so as to eliminate silos and improve the delivery of outcomes. This agile approach allows project teams to work in collaboration to ensure consistency in delivery, develop high-quality software that offers value for the business by implementing processes that are integrated all through the production stages.

A team was created that brought together design, development, and management teams. The development team included the development manager to offer team leadership and also brought on-board the operations managers and software architects to create an end-to-end project life cycle model.

IBM committed resources to train and mentor the new teams in agile and continuous delivery in all divisions of the company. IBM focused on capabilities against components of the product, which helped IBM to break down old-style silos and allow for collaboration and automation of processes. Specific managers were dedicated to managing the newly formed development team. Regular scrum meetings were held to discuss and solve emerging issues, track key parameters, analyze key data sets, and communicate sensitive information to team members.

A strategic product committee was later formed to improve the timeliness of market changes in project development priorities. The committee comprised of product managers, development supervisors, and owners of the business. The committee was tasked to:

- Prioritize user experiences for yearly releases and align with the project's long-term vision.

- Identify the long-term vision of the overall business.

- Manage, support, and assist in the execution of the project.

- Ensure that the project is fully funded to ensure the successful delivery of project objectives.

Leveraging Test Automation

Automation and virtualization were implemented using an agile and continuous testing approach in order to reduce lengthy back-end test cycles and improve the quality of releases. A schedule was created that included a four-week iteration that concluded with a demonstration and a four-week presentation of milestones that concluded with a release that a client could use.

Holding reflective meetings after each milestone helped IBM to eliminate waste in future projects. The motto that motivated the SWG team was "test early and test often."

The IBM SWG team implemented the following best practices for project automation:

- Run automation early and very often on every build.

- Automating processes that are prone to bugs.

- All routine and repetitive tasks were automated.

- Designed automation that does not interfere with user interface (UI) changes. The team created a framework that clearly separates the User interface from the tests.

- The team could constantly evaluate automation to hunt for bugs.

- Establish parameters that can assist evaluate whether automation is important or not in order to identify what to improve.

- Automation work was included in the overall work plan, and developers allowed time to work on project automation.

- The team made it easy to create, deliver, and maintain automation, thus making strong feature team ownership.

To provision for test automation, the SWG team deployed IBM's Rational Test Workbench for functional and performance testing, and to facilitate regular testing, build automation and deployment was critical. Implementation of the IBM UrbanCode enabled the test team to reduce the overall cost by 90% by using automated build deployment, which included apps and database server configuration settings.

Creating a DevOps Delivery Path

The SWG team decided to build a delivery path/pipeline that was pegged on the tool as a service approach to enable developers to commit code, deploy and test in an actual production environment in an hour as compared to previously when they could take one to two days to accomplish. This eliminated the need to rework and maximized overall productivity.

The established continuous delivery path incorporated the following best practices:

- Automating all processes where possible and using the shift-left approach.

- SWG team treated infrastructure as code.

- The team designed the code in such a manner that at any one time, it could be shipped (ship-readiness).

- The SWG team implemented the same deployment mechanism at all stages of development.

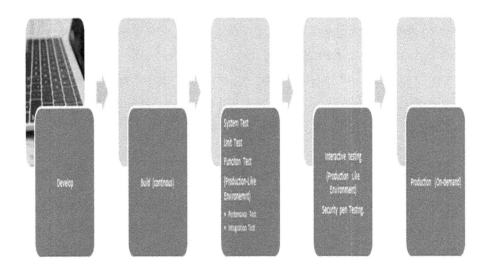

IBM's SWG Continuous project delivery pipeline.

In order to implement a continuous delivery pipeline, the developers should treat infrastructure as code. Here, the developers will use scripts to configure the needed infrastructure for the application to be part of the application code. Earlier, this procedure was carried out by system administrators or operations teams, but in the recent development, the control and efficiency it provides can be done directly by the developer. UrbanCode, Puppet, and Cheff are examples of the latest infrastructure automation tools implemented to make infrastructure as code real.

The SWG team treats infrastructure as a code by following a set of best practices borrowed from previous experiences and new software demands. The practices include:

- Cleaning up catalog resources to prevent sprawling.

- Automating the process of testing patterns.

- Handle pattern versions in multiple cloud platforms.

- Automating the process of deploying pattern topology in the cloud.

- Categorize all releases in versions.

- Treat services, pattern definition, and script packages as code.

Rapid Experimentation

DevOps concept of continuous delivery does not include software development activities only, other activities like continuous integration (CI) and Continuous Deployment (CD) are incorporated as key activities for learning. This kind of learning is achieved through regular experimentation and measuring the end results.

Once features and functionalities are added to an app, the developer will not be sure if the client will receive the envisioned benefits. It is for this reason that IBM often experiments early in the system development cycle and get feedback from clients as to what works well and ignore features that have little or no benefits to customers. Some features may even hinder the functionality of the system; this should be completely discarded. The figure below illustrates the experimentation strategy.

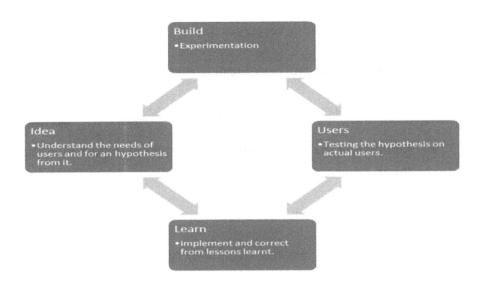

A Hypothesis-driven experimentation design.

The IBM SWG development team derived lots of lessons on frequent experimentation. Below are some of the lessons learned that were applied as best practices in future developments:

- They established parameters for success or failure.

- Established what worked well by running frequent experiments. This was carried out as small experiments on a sampled set of users to assist them in determining how useful a specific feature is.

- Simultaneously running experiments throughout the design process.

- Quickly deliver so as to experiment quickly immediately after delivery.

- The team established a mechanism to enable experimenting in the entire system, like Google Analytics and IBM Digital Analytics.

- Applied different models in experimenting, for instance, classical A/B tests and Multi-armed bandit.

- The team followed two paths at the same time for similar projects. They experimented on a cloud-based project and applied the resultant data from the experiments to steer the project in the right direction, including on-premise projects.

Improving Continuously (lean & agile principles)

The SWG team needed to create a culture of continuous improvement in order to leverage measures of effectiveness and efficiency to ensure that the process was improving. Agile principles were applied in attaining continuous improvement.

Continuous improvement was achieved by constantly tracking project goals, pressure points, and necessary actions required to solve the issues identified. Constant tracking ensures that the teams are constantly working towards a common goal and that the investment put in is understood widely. Project goals may require some period of time, say a quarter or more to develop and implement. Larger pressure points may take extended periods of months to lessen or completely eliminate them. It is good practice to limit all these measures within a month for efficient delivery of the project.

The team utilizes retrospectives to implement continuous improvement. Retrospective comprises regular reviews of what worked well for the team, what didn't, and the action necessary to improve. Failure to reflect on this means an important part of the project, and DevOps processes have not been accomplished. Complex teams may require a system of retrospective carried hierarchically. Here, each component team does a reflective exercise, and the findings are used as input into application-level reflection and then used in higher-level retrospective. Actions taken as a result of the reflection activities are often documented as pressure points with proposed improvement activities to take to reduce or completely eliminate the pressure or error points.

For the team to be certain that they are headed in the right direction, the team established business parameters and operational parameters to ensure that DevOps principles are applied effectively in the software development cycle. Business-related parameters include quantified improvements for the faster delivery time, improved customer satisfaction, minimized maintenance spending while at the same time increasing innovation investment, and increased adaptability by the customers.

Operational parameters directly affect the efficiency of the team over time and are quantified by looking at the time required to initiate a new project, time to build a project, and the duration for the iteration test.

Exploring DevOps Results

The SWG team used the DevOps approach to improve customer satisfaction, increase adaptability at the client-side, and increase enterprise revenue earnings. DevOps ensure short delivery time, resulting in rapid delivery of upgraded in house solutions and new cloud services like Bluemix, DevOps services for Bluemix, and collaborative lifecycle management as managed service (CLM aaMS).

Chapter Seven

Myths Surrounding DevOps

In this chapter, we will explore the myriad misconceptions surrounding DevOps and dispel the myths that indicate that DevOps will not work in some situations. You will understand what DevOps can do and what it is not meant for.

DevOps culture is an evolving culture that is still growing in magnitude and scope in organizations. Like any new concept or movement, DevOps has attracted a fair amount of Myths and fallacies. Most of these myths are coined by companies or organizations that have implemented DevOps without success.

Below are some of the 19 much-publicized misconceptions/myths about DevOps:

1. **That DevOps is only for online-based applications** – it is true DevOps originated from web-based companies like Etsy, Flickr, and Netflix that originated and resided on the internet, but this does not imply that DevOps principle can only be applied in the design of web-based applications. Many organizations have used DevOps principles to deliver software successfully. The continued improvement of the DevOps approach and principles have enabled companies to apply DevOps in many areas and teams in the respective

organizations. DevOps has been applied to technologies residing in multiple platforms, both cloud, and on-premise with distributed teams.

2. **That DevOps is the process of Operations team to learn how to code** – the operators have always been coding to manage development environments and routine tasks, but when infrastructure as code came in, the team appreciated the need to manage these codes using software engineering practices like versioning code, check-out, check-in, merging and branching. Nowadays, an improved version of the environment is created by the ops team by developing a new version of codes that defines it. This should not be confused to mean that the operations team needs to learn to code in Java or C++. Infrastructure as code tools utilizes programming languages like Ruby, which is easy to comprehend, especially for operators with a strong scripting background.

3. **That DevOps approach is only for Developers and Operators** – despite the fact that the name DevOps is a combination of the two terms 'Developers' and 'Operators,' it can be applied to all teams in software development. DevOps principles apply to quality assurance teams, management teams, business owners, practitioners, executives, project partners, suppliers, customers, among others. All these stakeholders have a stake in DevOps.

4. **That DevOps is not for ITIL** – some developers worry that the DevOps principles such as continuous delivery are discordant with the checks and processes prescribed by the Information Technology Infrastructure Library (ITIL), which comprises of a set of standard best practices for IT services management. ITIL model is totally compatible with DevOps. Almost all the principles of ITIL align perfectly with the principles of DevOps. Many organization does not adopt ITIL since it is based on the waterfall processes that do not encourage rapid changes and improvement. DevOps comes in to align these practices and bring harmony between development and operations.

    Many people view DevOps as a counterattack to ITIL or ITSM (IT service management) that was formulated back in the 80s. ITIL processes are compatible with DevOps processes, although DevOps support shorter lead time and higher deployment frequencies. Recently, ITIL processes are fully automated, thus solving problems associated with configuration and release management processes.

5. **That DevOps cannot be applied in regulated companies** – regulated sectors have the principal need for constant checks and balances and approvals from stakeholders at every stage to ensure compliance and auditability. Implementing DevOps improves compliance if handled in the right way. Automation tools can be used to design systems that have the in-built capability to capture audit logs.

Regulated industries or sectors can have several checkpoints for checking the integrity of the processes, but this does not mean that DevOps is incompatible with it.

6. **That DevOps cannot be applied for Outsources development projects** – Outsourcing is a common practice in all designed fields. In software development, outsourced teams are suppliers or capability providers in the DevOps delivery cycle. Organizations should ensure that the practices of the suppliers and other outsourced processes are compatible with the process used by the teams internally. This can be accomplished by having a common release plan, task management, and common asset repository tools to improve communication and collaboration between various teams and suppliers. If done well, this will greatly improve the organization's ability to define and coordinate the release procedure for all stakeholders.

7. **That DevOps only works on the cloud** – DevOps is synonymous to the cloud because of its inherent nature of existing on the internet and its ability to dynamically provision resources for developers and testers to rapidly obtain test environments on the cloud. Though, it doesn't mean that it must always be implemented on the cloud. Provided the company has efficient processes for hosting resources for deployment and testing of changes in applications. Working on a virtual environment is an optional feature. Continuous delivery can be achieved on on-

premise servers once they are configured to handle the same at high speeds.

8. **That DevOps cannot be used for Large and complex systems** – design of complex systems or software require high levels of discipline and close collaboration amongst the team players. These are principles that DevOps provides. Such complicated systems are usually made up of many software and hardware components, each with its own unique delivery cycle and timelines. DevOps can be applied to enhance coordination of these components and the system release plans.

9. **That DevOps handles only communication** – this misconception assumes that DevOps is meant only to handle communication during project design. It assumes that design problems can only be solved by effective communication amongst the stakeholders. This is not true since DevOps handles all levels of collaboration and associated communication plans in the entire cycle. Communication plays a major part in DevOps implementation coupled with agile and lean principles; it helps eliminates inefficient processes in the project cycle.

10. **That DevOps stands for continuous deployment** – this myth comes from companies that only deploy web-based applications. DevOps is not limited to deployment only, and most definitely, it's not just about continuous deployment. Implementing DevOps enables companies to release to the

production when they need to and not relying on a set calendar date.

11. **That DevOps is only for Start-up businesses** – DevOps was popularized by web-based startups like Google, Etsy, Amazon, and Netflix. This made people believe that DevOps was meant for startups. This is a misconception because DevOps is used globally by multinationals and established companies like IBM, Microsoft, among others.

DevOps culture helps to break down barriers in software development; it can help speed up software development and deployment, which is favorable for web-based companies or products that normally require to be developed and deployed faster compared to other products.

12. **That DevOps replaces Agile** – it is true that DevOps principles are compatible with Agile, but DevOps is no way meant to replace Agile. DevOps is meant to complement agile, which introduced in the year 2001. Agile is only a facilitator for DevOps since it focuses on small teams that deliver quality codes to its clients.

13. **That DevOps is not compatible with Information Security and Compliance** – The fact that DevOps lacks security controls in its principles has made people think that DevOps cannot be applied for the design of security-sensitive applications. DevOps systems have effective controls for security management. In DevOps, the security

checks and measured and constantly carried throughout the project cycle, unlike other methodologies where they are applied to the end product. This leads to the development of quality software with better security and compliance features.

14. **That DevOps was established to eliminate IT Operations** – some people look at DevOps as a methodology that is meant to eliminate traditional IT operations. However, this is not true. IT operations are very important in the implementation of DevOps. The two approaches often work in synergy as opposed to competing as insinuated by the myth. IT operations will be initiated earlier in the project before implementing the DevOps principles.

15. **That DevOps is applied only for Open Source software only** – the myth stems from the successful implementation of DevOps in open source software companies and products like Linux Apache, MySQL and PHP stack (LAMP) among others. It should be noted that the application of DevOps is independent of the underlying technology used.

16. **That DevOps is a job title** - recently, the job title of DevOps engineers has been complicated since they overlap with other jobs like system administrators. The overlaps occur when you have system administrators who can write codes and developers who know about system administration. Although it is not practical for an individual to be a full-time system admin and at the same time to be a

full-time developer since this will compromise the quality of his work, at the initial stages, it may be necessary to have the developers doing the deployment of the code and maintaining the systems; this is viable in cloud bases systems suitable for startups. As the company grows in complexity and size, it will not be possible to have the developers double up as operators. DevOps principles should be applied by everyone in the organization in order to realize efficient results.

17. **That you need DevOps certification to implement it** – as defined in chapter 1, DevOps is a cultural movement. It is practically impossible to certify culture. It is impossible to certify how effectively you communicate or collaborate with people or how well teams in your organization work together, and how your company learns. Certification is carried out on technologies that require some level of expertise to use, like the CISCO networking certification. DevOps does not have specific technology or- solutions.

18. **That DevOps is all about automation** – since DevOps principles are formulated around configuration management and continuous integration, you may tend to see DevOps as a way to automate software development processes and eliminate system administrators. Additionally, DevOps will lead people to think that anything that can be automated should be automated because of the existence of the DevOps methodology. DevOps is simply a culture that strives to get people working together. Automation is applied to repetitive

routine tasks only, which, if automated, will help free some time for them to engage in core activities. This increases the efficiency of handling software development processes. Automating server processes saves hours per server for the system admin. Globally, there has been a discussion on the role of automation in various industries and how human factors affect the elements that can be automated.

19. **That DevOps is a passing fad** – since DevOps is not a specific tool, technology, or method, it is likely to be replaced or become a passing whim. This should remain a myth because the tenets of DevOps are here to stay. The principles won which DevOps is based are solid and cannot be easily ignored in the software development world in the near future. A culture of improving the efficiency of project delivery, as well as staff satisfaction, cannot be a passing whim. Despite being similar to ITIL, Lean, and Agile in many ways, DevOps is a movement well-defined by ideas, not strict definitions like Agile. It is the continuous development of ideas behind DevOps that have managed to make it relevant until now and will likely be in existence for many years to come. There have been discussions recently on whether DevOps has lost its meaningfulness. Critics say what that DevOps is not rather than what it is, lack of conciseness in the definition. They also say that DevOps is just a rebranding of philosophies that came before it and that it will be discarded as soon as a new movement comes. In the past, people have been concerned about working in silos,

suggested continuous learning and improvement, advocated for automation, collaboration, and integration in the workplace. DevOps culture is the first movement to bring all these ideas together in a manner that the success of its implementation can be measured.

Conclusion

We have now reached the end of this educative book. We hope that you now have a clear understanding of DevOps and how you can apply its principle in your business in order to improve collaboration and communication in the software development cycle. Implementing DevOps, in the long run, gives your business a competitive advantage since it helps you to deliver quality products to your client and in record time.

It is impossible to have a competitive advantage when your business' operations are centralized and not to evolve at all. Throughout the book, we have explored how to integrate operations into the daily tasks of development and discussed how to monitor progress continuously by automating routine design processes.

Organizations that apply the DevOps approach will report fewer failures, and if they fail, they will recover faster and have a motivated staff. In siloed working environments, lack of a common understanding of the organization's objectives leads to the delivery of substandard products and extended lead time. The concepts and principles that will help an organization achieve this have been discussed in detail in the chapters in this book.

In the next book, we will discuss further the pillars for effective DevOps, namely collaboration, hiring staff, Affinity, scaling, and tools that were introduced in this book. In the next book, each pillar will be discussed in its entirety with practical examples from a diverse set of companies, from web startups to large companies that have fully adopted the DevOps methodology.

www.ingramcontent.com/pod-product-compliance
Lightning Source LLC
Chambersburg PA
CBHW071135050326
40690CB00008B/1467